God's
Answers
to Human
Dilemmas

God's Answers to Human Dilemmas

Larry Kennedy

Broadman Press
Nashville, Tennessee

© Copyright 1980 • Broadman Press
All rights reserved.

4251-73
ISBN: 0-8054-5173-0

Dewey Decimal Classification: 248.4
Subject heading: CHRISTIAN LIFE

Library of Congress Catalog Card Number: 79-66206
Printed in the United States of America

Dedication

To my wife, Marty
and my sons
Steve and Scott

Contents

About the Author

Dr. Larry Wells Kennedy is pastor of the First Baptist Church of Laurel, Mississippi. Born in Lousiana, he was reared in Pensacola, Florida.

He was educated at Lousiana College (B.A.), New Orleans Baptist Theological Seminary (Th.M.), and Mississippi State University (M.A., Ph.D.). He began the ministry at nineteen and has pastored Manifest Baptist Church, Manifest, Louisiana, Mantee Baptist Church, Mantee, Mississippi, and First Baptist Church, Amory, Mississippi, prior to becoming pastor at Laurel.

He is married to the former Martha G. Guinn of Jonesville, Louisiana. The Kennedys have two sons, Jon Stephen and Michael Scott.

Dr. and Mrs. Kennedy have received a number of academic and civic honors. Mrs. Kennedy was "Miss Louisiana College." Dr. Kennedy has preached in Europe, Africa, the Middle East, and South America. He is active in community and denominational life. He appears in the 1975 edition of *Outstanding Young Men of America.* His first book with Broadman was *Down with Anxiety!*

1

When the Innocent Suffer

Exodus 1:1-14; 2:23-25

With the rise of a new political regime in Egypt, the Hebrews lost their middle-class standing in society and were forced into slavery. The Bible states: "The Egyptians compelled the sons of Israel to labor rigorously; and they made their lives bitter with hard labor in mortar and bricks and at *all kinds* of labor in the field, all their labors which they rigorously imposed on them" (Ex. 1:13-14). I am sure that most of the Hebrews asked, "Lord, why is this happening to us? What have we done to deserve this treatment?"

Oradour-Sur-Glane is a small village in France. Very few people have ever heard of it; however, it has something to say about suffering. On June 10, 1944, two trucks filled with Nazi soldiers rolled into the village. In another section of France, the French underground had killed a German officer. For reasons known only to the German command, it was decided that 50 persons in this village would be killed in retaliation. At the last minute the officer in charge of the executions decided that 50 deaths were not enough; he proceeded to execute every man, woman, and child in the village. The men were taken to the barns and machine-gunned, and then the barns were set afire. The women and children were taken to the church and all were shot. The church was burned to the ground. When the shooting stopped 642 people, 254 of them children, were dead.

9

One person managed to survive the holocaust, Madame Marguerite Rouffange. She saw her little boy, two daughters, seven-month-old grandchild, and her husband shot and burned. She was shot five times, but she managed to crawl out of the burning church into the nearby forest. Today Madame Rouffange refuses to be photographed or interviewed by the press. What little is known about the holocaust has come from her neighbors, who occasionally have picked up small pieces of information from her in private conversations. No one lives in the village today, and it exists as a monument to suffering. I wonder how many times Madame Rouffange has asked, Why?

Today in the Soviet Union, China, Uganda, and other places around the world, Christians are experiencing suffering similar to that recorded in Exodus 1. They, too, are probably asking, Why, God? For these Christians the book of Exodus is a reflection of their own experiences. It could be that you are in the midst of suffering. As we ask, Why? let us study this text and seek to apply it to our lives. Notice these characteristics of the people of God.

The People of God Were Suffering

The Hebrews, whose ancestors had settled in Egypt under the leadership of Joseph and had enjoyed complete freedom, became a persecuted minority. A new pharaoh came to power who was jealous of their strength and decided to place them in bondage. In a short period of time the Hebrews were forced into slavery and suffered extreme persecution.

How are we to understand this suffering? It has been suggested by some that this suffering was sent by God. Those who suggest that God was the author of this suffering contend that he sent it in order to develop character in the lives of his people. According to this view, these hardships made them a better people. Some people believe that God sent the suffering in order to prepare the Hebrews for Canaan. The hardships of Egypt gave them a deeper appreciation for the Promised Land. A few sincere Bible students believe that God sent the suffering in order to punish the Hebrews for past sins. This viewpoint contends that the descendants of Jacob's children were compelled to suffer for the past sin of selling Joseph into slavery.

A second reason given for this suffering is the work of the devil. Certainly the book of Job indicates that Satan had his hand in the suffering of God's people. Without a doubt he was active when the Hebrews felt the cruel hand of tyranny. When God's children are persecuted, one can be sure that the devil is very near.

The sinfulness of men is often given as the reason for the Hebrews' suffering. The envy and jealousy that lurked in the heart of Pharaoh was a key factor in this suffering. The world has always had its Hitlers and Stalins and will continue to have them in the days to come.

Although the church in America has not known widespread persecution because of religious beliefs, Christians experience some form of suffering every day. In the face of suffering, we must be honest enough to say that we do not always know why God's people suffer. As I have stood with other believers in the midst of intense suffering, I have not always had an answer as to why the suffering came; however, I have had a promise that has meant much to me and to those who have suffered. The promise is, "I consider that the sufferings of this present time are not worthy to be compared with the glory that is to be revealed to us" (Rom. 8:18).

The apostle Paul and the early church knew what it was to suffer for Christ's sake. In many ways their suffering was similar to that of the Hebrews in Egypt. The wise apostle was quick to observe that God's people are not immune to suffering. Many times a commitment to God guarantees suffering. Paul's writings remind us, as he reminded the believers of his day, that faithfulness has its reward. The suffering of this age is only temporary, and in the end God will receive us into his eternal presence.

The People of God Were Strengthened

The text that we are studing says that in the midst of the suffering the Hebrews multiplied and grew stronger (see Ex. 1:12). The new pharaoh had sought to break the people of God, but he soon discovered that they had an indomitable will to live. They refused to renounce their faith in God. The lashes of the whips and the curses of the overseers simply intensified their prayers to God.

I have noticed that people react to adversity in one of two ways: They either become bitter or better. Some believers throw up their hands and give in to self-pity; others discover new courage and become more Godlike in character. It could be that faithfulness in the face of suffering is the key to becoming more like our heavenly Father.

Recently I read the book *Joni*. It is the story of a young girl who is paralyzed from the neck down because of a swimming accident. In the beginning she asked God many times why this had happened to her, but out of this suffering, she found God in a new and deeper way. After hearing her speak, I saw firsthand how Christlike she really is. I was literally overwhelmed by the Spirit of Christ that emanated from her personality. Her faithfulness in the midst of her suffering has strengthened her commitment to Christ and has given her a spiritual power that few Christians enjoy.

The record of the early church, as revealed in the book of Acts would indicate that suffering can be a stepping-stone to spiritual power. Stephen and other persecuted Christians were aglow with the Spirit of Christ, and God used them in spreading the gospel. All of this reminds us that, even out of the most intense suffering, God is able to bring good. The promise of Romans 8:37 is valid: "But in all these things we overwhelmingly conquer through Him who loved us." God really does make a difference when suffering comes to our door.

Father Damien was a Belgian missionary who went to Hawaii to work with the lepers on the island of Moloka. There were over six hundred lepers, and he became their spiritual guide. Because he was the only healthy person, he felt alone. One morning, while pouring hot water, he accidentally spilled some on his feet. He felt no pain. Instantly, he realized that it meant he, too, was a leper. A strange joy filled his heart. Running to the church, he rang the church bell calling the other lepers to worship. When all had arrived, he leaped into his pulpit and shouted with joy, "Fellow lepers, fellow lepers." Yes, when suffering comes, we can be conquerors through Jesus Christ.

The People of God Were Supplicating

What do you do when you are suffering? What do you do when a loved one is hurting? We have several choices: become angry with God and others, indulge in self-pity, give up on life, or pray and trust God.

Most of us turn to prayer as a last resort. Only when we get desperate do we consider God. Having decided to pray, we usually seek God for only a few minutes over a period of a few weeks. Have you ever considered a prayer request that might be continued by your great-grand-children? The Bible tells us that God's people in Egypt prayed for four hundred years, asking God to deliver them from suffering. I have a feeling that they really meant business with God. Apparently prayer not only prepared the way for God to act but it also enabled the Hebrews to cope with the adversity they were experiencing.

The Bible declares that prayer is one means whereby we receive strength to cope with all that life may bring our way. The example of Jesus in the garden before his death, Paul's prayer recorded in 2 Corinthians 12, and Stephen's prayer for forgiveness recorded in Acts 7 all reveal that prayer enabled these men to find victory in the midst of suffering.

When we are willing to pray in the midst of suffering, several things will become evident. First, prayer gives expression to a living faith. In the prayer parables of Luke 18:1-8, Jesus made it clear that when he returns he will look for those whose faith was expressed in prayer. Second, God uses our prayers as a witness to his realness. The continual praying of the Hebrews must have caused much consternation among the Egyptians. Through daily prayer the Hebrews gave witness that their faith was genuine. Third, prayer gives strength to the one praying. Only fools seek suffering; however, when suffering comes, prayer is the key to finding victory in the midst of it.

The teacup looked like an ordinary teacup until it spoke:

"You do not understand. I have not always been a teacup. There was a time when I was nothing but red clay. My master took me, rolled me, and patted me over and over and over. I yelled, 'Leave me alone!' But he only smiled and said, 'Not yet.' Then I was placed on a spinning wheel and spun around and around. I screamed, 'Stop it! I am getting dizzy.' The master nodded and said, 'Not yet.' Then he put me in an oven, and it was terribly hot. I thought he would burn me to a crisp. I yelled and knocked on the door. I could see his lips moving as he said, 'Not yet.' Finally, the door was opened and I began to cool. Then suddenly he painted me all over, and the fumes were horrible. I cried, 'Stop it! Stop it!' He only nodded: 'Not yet.' All at once he put me back in the oven, and it was twice as hot. I begged, pleaded, screamed, and cried. But he only said, 'Not yet.' Then at the last minute, just when I knew I would never make it, he opened the oven and placed me on a shelf. An hour later he handed me a mirror and said, 'Look at your self.' I was beautiful, really beautiful.

"As I gazed at my beauty, my master said: 'I know it hurt to be rolled and patted, but if I had left, you would have dried up. I know it hurt to be spun around and around. But if I had stopped, you would have crumbled. I know it hurt in the oven, but if I had stopped you would have cracked. I know the fumes were bad when I painted you, but if I had stopped you never would have hardened. But now you are a finished product. You are what I had in mind when I first began with you!'"[1]

We do not always know why we have to suffer. However, when we trust God in the midst of our suffering, he is able to make us stronger persons. God can turn our suffering into victory. Yes, when we have reached the end of the rope, it is time to tie a knot and hang on.

2

A Girl Named Jochebed

Exodus 2:1-10; Numbers 26:59

You are single. A friend of yours informs you that he would like for you to date a new girl who has just arrived in town. In the past you have made it a practice never to go out on blind dates, but your friend has aroused your curiosity. He tells you that this new girl is very attractive and that her father is very wealthy. Being a fellow who has always appreciated beauty and wealth, you believe that this new girl might be an interesting date. So you ask your friend for her name. He replies, "Jochebed." Common sense tells you that no one needs to date a girl with that name.

Thousands of years ago there was a young girl named Jochebed, and a young Hebrew boy found her very attractive. She became the jewel of his heart, and he took her for his wife. His choice was a wise one because history would later demonstrate that she would be the mother of three of the greatest leaders in the history of the Hebrew people. The Scripture states: The name of Amram's wife was Jochebed, the daughter of Levi, who was born to Levi in Egypt; "and she bore to Amram: Aaron and Moses and their sister Miriam" (Num. 26:59).

In this text, God is teaching us three important truths.

The Family Exerts Tremendous Influence

Among many people today there is great concern about the deterioration of the family because the family unit has

17

always been the backbone of productive civilizations. Civilizations and nations have thrived when the family unit was healthy and have crumbled when the family unit decayed. When the family unit has taught positive values and exhibited genuine love, strength, courage, and integrity have been obvious by-products.

Although Moses seemingly had little contact in his early years with his Hebrew family, their limited influence greatly affected his life. His mother's decision to place him in the Nile was an act of faith (Heb. 11:23). She offered him up to God, believing that God could do what she could not. Surely she must have continually prayed for him as Miriam gave daily reports concerning his activities in the house of Pharaoh. The Scriptures imply that Moses was not totally ignorant of his Hebrew background and probably was greatly affected in his adolescent years by the sincere faith of his Hebrew family.

Samuel was a great prophet of God. The Word declares that the faith of his mother was a contributing factor in his spiritual development. His mother, Hannah, had prayed earnestly for a child. She promised God that if she ever gave birth she would "give him to the Lord all the days of his life" (1 Sam. 1:11). At one time her praying was so intense that the old priest Eli thought she was drunk. He was tempted to banish her from his presence until he realized that she was pouring out her soul to God. Samuel was a force for good in ancient Israel, and his family exerted a tremendous influence upon his life.

In praising Timothy, the apostle Paul wrote:"I am mindful of the sincere faith within you, which first dwelt in your grandmother Lois, and your mother Eunice, and I am sure that *it is* in you as well" (2 Tim. 1:5). The apostle was hopeful that young Timothy would carry on the work of spreading the gospel. Sensing that his death was near,

Paul believed Timothy would continue that which Paul had initiated. As he reflected on Timothy's life, the wise missionary saw what a tremendous influence Timothy's family had played in his spiritual development. The astute Paul was confident that Timothy's family background would provide solid foundation for a dynamic preacher.

Moses, Samuel, and Timothy remind all of us that a godly family does exert a positive influence upon the lives of God's people.

Faith Is Powerful

The Scripture states: "By faith Moses, when he was born, was hidden for three months by his parents, because they saw he was a beautiful child; and they were not afraid of the king's edict" (Heb. 11:23). The faith mentioned in this text is not the faith of Moses, but the faith of his parents.

By faith men trust God and refuse to give up even when they do not understand what God is doing. Surely Jochebed was confused and distressed at knowing that her child would be killed. In all probability she asked God, "Why?" Even though she did not understand God's plan, she put her child into God's will. By God's plan he was rescued from the Nile and reared in Pharaoh's house. I have often wondered what Hebrew name Jochebed would have given Moses. I have wondered how many sleepless nights she spent pondering the fact that her son was in the palace, that she could never go and embrace him. However, by faith she had said, "I refuse to quit." When she had reached the end of her rope, she tied a knot and hung on.

Jochebed reminds us that faith involves more than believing a lot of facts about God. Genuine faith involves obedience, trust, and a willingness not to give up even when God's will is unknown or contrary to our own desires. Faith is trusting God in the midst of much suffering and heartache. Because of the faith of Jochebed, God exhibited his power in the life of Moses, and world history was dramatically changed.

Dr. Robert Schuller, pastor of the Garden Grove Community Church, Garden Grove, California, learned from his father that real faith never capitulates to evil circumstances. One afternoon he and his father were sitting on the front porch of their farm house in Iowa. All at once a dark cloud gathered on the horizon. As it moved closer, a rumbling sound like numerous freight trains could be heard. Out of the darkness a long, gray funnel cloud hit the ground, swirling its way toward the Schuller farm. The family knew a tornado was about to hit. Gathering his family, Elder Schuller jumped into his car and raced away a safe distance. From a nearby hill they watched the tornado pass. Just as quickly as it appeared, the tornado was gone.

Although they knew the storm had been destructive, they were not prepared for what they found upon returning home. The Schuller farm had consisted of nine buildings, and not one was left. The moans of dying cattle pierced the air, and Robert Schuller's prize horse was dead with a fourteen-foot-long two-by-four in its belly.

Elder Schuller had worked for twenty-six years trying to pay off the mortgage. With tears in his eyes he looked at his wife and said, "Jennie, it's all gone; it's all gone! Twenty-six years, and it's all gone in ten minutes!" Elder Schuller got out of the car and walked across the land that was his farm. A little while later he returned to the car and in his hand was a small plaque that had hung in the kitchen. The words of the plaque were, "Keep looking to

Jesus." Elder Schuller decided right then that he would look to Jesus and not give up.

Most of the farmers of the area left, deciding not to rebuild. With faith in God, Elder Schuller started from scratch and within five years he had a new farm that was debt free. He was a man who understood that faith involves trusting God and refusing to give up even when the future looks bleak. He was made of the same stuff as Jochebed.[1]

Because of a personal problem, do you feel like quitting? A father was trying desperately to build confidence in his son. With sympathy in his voice the father said, "Son, don't ever give up, never quit."

The boy responded, "But, Dad, I simply can't do it!"

The father said, "Always remember, my son, the people who are remembered are those who refused to quit. Robert Fulton never quit. Thomas Edison never gave up. Eli Whitney never gave up—and look at Isadore McPringle."

The boy exclaimed, "Who in the world is Isador McPringle?"

"See," said the father, "You have never heard of him. He gave up."[2]

Yes, anybody can throw up his hands in despair and quit. However, when you are willing to put your faith in the Lord, he will give you the strength to live victoriously in the midst of your problems. When you have reached the end of your rope, tie a knot and hang on.

The Future of God's People Is Indestructible

The plan of God can never be defeated. The Nile River was a god to the Egyptians. In all probability the throwing of the Hebrew children into the river was a form of sacrifice to one of the Egyptian deities. From the very spot where Satan sought to hurt the Hebrews, God rescued Moses and anointed him for leadership. The devil intended to bring much evil upon God's people, but the Lord took a bad situation and brought good from it.

Romans 8:28 states: "We know that God causes all things to work together for good to those who love God." This verse does not say that everything that happens to us is good. Romans 8:28 does remind us that God is able to bring good out of bad situations for those people who love him and refuse to quit. Certainly that truth is demonstrated as God delivered Moses and used him as a vessel of God's power. God has a plan to bring good to you even in the midst of all your suffering. Don't give up! In a leprosarium in Japan, a blind leper decided that he wanted to learn to read; however, he could not use the Braille system because leprosy had destroyed the sense of touch in his hands. Refusing to give up, he attempted to learn to read Braille with his toes; but the feeling was gone from his toes. Finally he remembered he had one sensitive part of his body still intact. Today he reads his Braille Bible with his tongue.[3]

The religious leaders who stoned Stephen (Acts 7) thought they were putting an end to Christianity. God took that tragic act and used it as the church scattered, preaching the gospel. Stephen's death had a great influence on the conversion of Paul. Stephen's death reminds us of how God can bring good out of tragic circumstances. His plans for his people are never defeated. What looks like defeat to us is simply God's highway to victory.

Paul and Silas were thrown in jail for preaching the gospel (Acts 16). Out of that difficult situation God was able to work through Paul and Silas to change the heart of a jailer. The devil intended much evil when he had Paul and Silas thrown in prison; God was present to bring about good. The conversion of the Philippian jailer reminds us of the indestructibility of God's plan for his people. When human circumstances are difficult, God has the opportunity to work miracles.

A hardworking Chinese farmer awoke one morning to discover that his only horse had escaped from the corral. His neighbors came to see him and said, "Your horse got loose! What bad luck!"

The farmer responded, "How do you know it's bad luck?" Sure enough, the next day the horse returned leading twelve other horses into the corral. Instead of having one horse, the farmer had thirteen.

His neighbors returned and said, "What good luck! You now have thirteen horses."

The farmer said, "How do you know it's good luck?" The following day the old man's son attempted to ride one of the new horses, but he fell and broke his leg.

The neighbors returned and said, "What bad luck!"

The farmer said, "How do you know it's bad luck?" Sure enough the next day a warlord came through the countryside and conscripted all the able-bodied young men for his army; the farmer's son was left because of his broken leg.

Yes, what looks like a tragedy to us, just might be a blessing from God. When human circumstances are difficult, God has the opportunity to work miracles. Jochebed was a Hebrew woman who put her faith in God. She reminds us that when we have reached the end of our rope, it is time to tie a knot and hang on.

3
The Hard Way

Exodus 2:11-14

Sometimes we learn important lessons about life the hard way. Recently, our three-year-old son was playing with the cigarette lighter in our car. We stopped him, explaining that the lighter was dangerous and could burn his hand. He listened silently and promised never again to touch the lighter. A few days later, while my wife was putting groceries in the house, she heard Steve screaming at the top of his lungs. Rushing back to the car, she discovered that he had pulled out the lighter and had touched the hot coils. Needless to say, he had learned the hard way not to play with cigarette lighters.

This Scripture reference does not tell us how Moses knew about his Hebrew background. The text simply says that "he went out to his brethren and looked on their hard labors" (Ex. 2:11). Miriam may have been able to maintain close contact with Moses, since she assisted the Egyptian maiden in bringing him into Pharaoh's house. In secret sessions at certain intervals, Miriam may have instructed Moses in his Hebrew heritage. It is also possible that the Egyptians reared Moses by making it clear to him that he was an adopted son. Influenced by his Hebrew heritage, he killed an Egyptian who was beating a Hebrew slave. He buried the body but soon discovered that the Hebrews and the Egyptians were aware of his deed. In fear he fled Egypt and escaped into the desert. He had to learn some truths the hard way.

Two Wrongs Never Make a Right

When Moses discovered an Egyptian beating a Hebrew slave, he struck out in anger and killed the Egyptian. Murder was not the answer to acts of cruelty, and God's future prophet learned the hard way that two wrongs never make a right.

Jesus taught this simple truth. In Luke 9:51-56, the Samaritans would have nothing to do with Jesus "because his face was set toward Jerusalem" (v. 51). James and John were indignant at the attitude of the Samaritans and suggested to Jesus that they should pray for fire to fall from heaven upon the Samaritans. If we had been there, we probably would have made the same suggestion. The Word of God states that Jesus "turned and rebuked them" (Luke 9:55).

When Jesus was arrested, Peter was disturbed to the point of cutting off the ear of a slave of the high priest. Jesus quickly responded by healing the slashed ear and said, "Stop! No more of this" (Luke 22:51). Jesus taught his disciples, in word and deed, that two wrongs never make a right.

The apostle Paul wrote about how to react when confronting evil:

Never pay back evil for evil to anyone. Never take your own revenge, beloved, but leave room for the wrath of God, for it is written, ". . . I WILL REPAY, SAYS THE LORD." Do not be overcome by evil, but overcome evil with good (Rom. 12:17,19,21).

These wise words remind us that if we answer a wrong with a wrong, we are simply allowing evil to become a part of our lives. In the end, the evil we sought to destroy will destroy us.

Several years ago I read about a father who took vengeance into his own hands. His oldest daughter rebelled and started associating with young people who were involved in drugs and sexual promiscuity. Late one night the police called to inform the father that his daughter had been found dead from an overdose of drugs. In a state of rage, the father loaded his rifle and drove to the house where his daughter had been living. Finding her "friends" at the house, he shot them all. If we had been in his place, we might have been tempted to do the same; however, two wrongs never make a right.

Nine-year-old Marcia Trimble was kidnapped and brutally murdered. A reporter once asked Mrs. Trimble, "If you could face the kidnapper, what would you say?"

She hesitated and then said, "I would tell him that God loves him." Mrs. Trimble is a Christian who, with God's help, has refused to allow evil to destroy her spirit. She knows that two wrongs never make a right.[1]

In 1970, Diane Bristol of San Diego, California, was raped and murdered. Out of the hurt and pain of that tragedy Diane's mother, Mrs. Goldie Mae Bristol, turned to God and was converted. Recently Mrs. Bristol spoke to a group of prisoners, saying that she had found the strength not only to forgive but also to love the young man responsible for her daughter's death. She was aware that her daughter's murderer was among the prisoners she was speaking to. At the conclusion of her talk, Michael Dennis Keeyes, the convicted killer of Mrs. Bristol's daughter, rose from his chair and walked forward to identify himself. His voice breaking, he tried to express his gratitude to Mr. and Mrs. Bristol. Later that day Michael Keeyes and the Bristols met in private. In trying to explain her attitude to the press, Mrs. Bristol said, "I can't explain it. I know others can't understand. Maybe it is best that way."[2] With God's help the Bristols had overcome evil with good, and they answered a wrong with a right.

"Amos and Andy" was truly one of the great TV comedies of all time. In one episode, Andy had grown tired of the abuse he was receiving from Kingfish. Kingfish would tell a joke and then slap Andy extremely hard across the chest. Speaking to Amos, Andy said, "I'm ready for the Kingfish." Throwing open his coat, he revealed several sticks of dynamite tied to his chest. He said, "The next time the Kingfish hit me, he gonna get his hand blown off." Andy was forgetting, however, that such an act would also blow a hole in his chest. Like Moses, he was on the verge of learning that two wrongs never make a right.

One night in 1958, a Korean student at the University of Pennsylvania was brutally murdered by a gang of teenagers. The citizens of Philadelphia cried for vengeance and demanded the death penalty. As the trial got under way, the district attorney received a letter from the parents and relatives of the murdered Korean student. The letter stated:

Our family has met together and we have decided to petition that the most generous treatment possible within the laws of your government be given to those who have committed this criminal act. We have decided to save money to start a fund to be used for the religious, educational, vocational, and social guidance of the boys when they are released. We have dared to express our hope with the spirit received from the gospel of our Saviour Jesus Christ, who died for our sins.[3]

Yes, the Bible says, "Do not be overcome by evil, but overcome evil with good" (Rom. 12:21).

A Hole in the Ground Will Not Cover Sin

After killing the Egyptian, Moses attempted to hide his deed. Digging a deep hole, he buried the dead man. Fearing detection and possible punishment, he assumed that burying the body would conceal the murder. However, his tragic deed was known, and he discovered the hard way that a hole in the ground cannot cover sin.

This act of Moses causes us to ask a simple question: How shall we cover our sins? Luke 18:9-14 tells of the Pharisee who denied his own sinfulness. The Pharisee was heard to say, "God, I thank Thee that I am not like other people: swindlers, unjust, adulterers, or even like this tax-gatherer" (Luke 18:11). This attempt to cover sin was futile. Jesus contended that a man who prayed in that manner was living an illusion. The apostle John put it best when he said, "If we say that we have no sin, we are deceiving ourselves, and the truth is not in us" (1 John 1:8). To deny your sinfulness is to guarantee that you will have a permanent seat in hell.

When confronted by God in the Garden of Eden, Adam and Eve attempted to deal with sin by blaming others. Adam blamed Eve, and Eve blamed the snake. They discovered that God would not allow them to "pass the buck." They could not cover their sin by blaming others.

Judas sought to escape his sin in suicide. Throughout history men and women have turned to this course of action; but it has never been the answer to sin. Suicide does not separate us from our responsibility to God, and it can never cover sin.

At times our attempts to cover our sins can be amusing. In 1875, J. P. Wofford was serving as pastor of the Mount Pleasant Baptist Church, Webster County, Mississippi. At the end of the cotton season, several members of the church rode in their wagons to West Point, Mississippi, to

sell their cotton. While in West Point, they all got drunk
and had trouble getting back to the Mount Pleasant community. Upon hearing of the incident, the Reverend Wofford prepared a hell-fire sermon on the evils of alcohol.
Wofford was so persuasive in his delivery that one member in the congregation jumped up and with tears in his
eyes cried, "Brother Wofford, don't you ever send me to
West Point any more to get your whiskey." Wofford later
claimed that the whiskey had been medicine for his wife,
Peggy.

The Bible tells us how our sins can be covered. The
apostle John wrote: "If we confess our sins, He is faithful
and righteous to forgive us our sins and to cleanse us from
all unrighteousness" (1 John 1:9). Our sins can only be
covered by the blood of Christ. When we come to Christ,
confessing our sinfulness, his death on the cross becomes
our mercy seat where our sins are covered by his blood (1
John 2:2).

Seaborn McKelva Cole, who preached immediately
after the Civil War, was one of the great Baptist preachers
of northeast Mississippi. Before the war Seaborn was
known for his riotous living and heavy drinking. His conversion occurred at the Battle of Gettysburg. As a member
of Company K of the Forty-second Mississippi Regiment,
he participated in Pickett's charge on the last day of the
great battle. Reaching the crest of Cemetery Ridge, Seaborn was wounded in the arm. By that time, the battle had
turned against the Confederates, and Rebel troops were
fleeing for their lives. Running as fast as his legs would
carry him, Seaborn attempted to escape the enemy's fire.
When he was about halfway down the hill, he was struck
in the eye. As he fell to his knees, he felt blood cover his
face. He looked to heaven and cried, "Lord, I'm a sinner.
Please forgive me." He then got up and struggled down

the hill. Again he was struck by a minie ball; the shock threw him to the ground. This time he looked to heaven and said, "Lord, if you will help me get off this hill, I will not only get saved, I'll be a preacher." God spared Seaborn's life, and he was one of the few survivors of Pickett's charge.

Because of sins, mistakes, and errors in judgment, we, too, are often forced to learn the hard way. If this has been your experience, don't be discouraged. Remember that God loves you and can use any learning experience to make your life rich and more useful in his service. Confess your mistakes, and seek God's will for your life.

4

Sin, What Then?

Exodus 2:11-14

In the previous chapter, we considered the attempt of Moses to cover his sin. Since sin is a critical problem to the human race, let us pursue this experience in the life of Moses more closely. How is man to deal with his sins? This question is as old as the human race. Men have struggled with this question and have offered many answers. This question has been the theme of the poet, the novelist, and the playwright. It has been the speculation of the philosopher and the unspoken thought of your next-door neighbor.

Sin and guilt are devastating forces that cripple the mind and waste the body. In the Shakespearean play, *Macbeth,* Lady Macbeth commits murder, then goes into a deep depression. Macbeth seeks out the doctor and says:

> Cure her of that:
> Canst thou not minister to a mind diseas'd;
> Pluck from the memory a rooted sorrow;
> Raze out the written troubles of the brain;
> And with some sweet oblivious antidote
> Cleanse the stuff'd bosom of that perilous stuff
> Which weighs upon the heart?[1]

Succinctly the doctor replies that there is no medical antidote for the problem that plagues Lady Macbeth. Her spiritual need is beyond his healing power.

In describing the cancer of sin and guilt, the poet wrote:

> The ghosts of forgotten actions
>   Come flocking before my sight,
> And the things that I thought were dead things
>   were alive with a terrible might.
> And the vision of all my past life
>   was a dreadful thing to face
> Alone, alone with my conscience
>   in that strange and fearful place.

The problem of sin is the problem of every man. How can man cover his sins? How can he deal with guilt? Is there an antidote for this "perilous stuff"?

Blaming Others

We can attempt to deal with our sins by blaming our sins on others. This is probably the oldest method man uses in attempting to deal with his sins. This is the approach that Adam and Eve took when God confronted them with their rebellion. The Bible states that God asked,

"Who told you that you were naked? Have you eaten from the tree of which I commanded you not to eat?" And the man said, "The woman whom Thou gavest to be with me, she gave me from the tree, and I ate." Then the LORD God said to the woman, "What is this you have done?" And the woman said, "The serpent deceived me, and I ate" (Gen. 3:11-13).

When God confronted Adam and Eve with their rebellion, Adam blamed Eve; Eve blamed the snake. In one sense Adam blamed God by implying that, because God had created woman, the Lord was a part of the problem. Ever since that experience when God's Garden was turned into a cesspool, man has been trying to pass the buck.

When failure comes to a marriage, partners easily blame each other for all the problems. The counselor hears the oft-repeated phrase: "I know I have my faults, but she (he) is. . . ." When children fail, they usually blame their parents; the parents blame the schools.

When we are seeking scapegoats, we conveniently blame "society." Recently, a young man in New Orleans killed several people indiscriminately. When the young man's mother was confronted with her son's terrible crimes, she went into a rage, blaming society for her son's sins.

As long as there are people on the earth, man will attempt to blame others for his sins. The tragedy is that such an approach will never solve the problem of guilt. It simply creates more problems.

Refusing Responsibility

We can attempt to deal with our sins by contending that our sinful conduct was really beyond our control. This is another way of saying that we are not responsible for our actions. Aaron, the brother of Moses, claimed his sin was beyond his control. In Exodus 32, the Bible states that Moses came down from the mountain of God and discovered that the people had made a golden calf for an idol. When he confronted Aaron, his brother replied,

"Do not let the anger of my lord burn; you know the people yourself, that they are prone to evil. . . . I said to them, 'Whoever has any gold, let them tear it off.' So they gave *it* to me, and I threw it into the fire, and out came this calf" (Ex. 32:22,24).

He simply added a lie to his other sins.

We laugh to ourselves as we ponder the ludicrous statement of Aaron; however, the tragedy of it all is that the human race is daily refusing responsibility for sin. Like

Aaron, men have claimed their idols of rebellion are being molded by invisible forces which are beyond human control.

During the trial of Jesus, Pilate realized that the evidence pointed to innocence; but the Roman governor was more politician than statesman. The pressure of the group was too much for him. Attempting to absolve himself of guilt, "he took water and washed his hands in front of the multitude, saying, 'I am innocent of this man's blood; see *to that* yourselves' " (Matt. 27:24). It was a futile attempt to cover his sin.

Are you attempting to deal with your sins in the manner of Aaron and Pilate? If you are, you are creating more problems for yourself.

Suppression

We can attempt to deal with our sins through suppression. Bringing all of our brain cells into operation, we can bury our sinful acts deep within the murky ground of the subconscious. King David appearately attempted to do this. Having committed adultery and murder, he continued his duties as God's anointed. However, God always has a way of bringing the past to the present. In the case of David, the prophet Nathan shared a parable with the king, revealing how a rich man had taken the only sheep of a poor man. David was indignant and demanded punishment for the culprit. Nathan responded, "You are the man! You have struck down Uriah the Hittite with the sword, have taken his wife to be your wife" (2 Sam. 12:7,9).

Some folks are able to suppress past sins for long periods of time. However, a common event can bring the suppressed sin to the forefront of one's mind, compounding the guilt and depression. Suppression is not the answer to sin.

Suicide

We can attempt to deal with our sins through suicide. Having betrayed Jesus, Judas "threw the pieces of silver into the sanctuary and departed; and he went away and hanged himself" (Matt. 27:5). For Judas the way out of guilt was the hanging tree.

Ernest Hemingway was a prolific writer. His contribution to literature is immense. He lived by the code of wine, women, and song. *Playboy* magazine applauded Hemingway's carefree life and contended that the great author had demonstrated that a little "sin" never hurt anyone. However, the serenity on Hemingway's face was not matched by a comparable tranquility in his soul. One day, while in his mountain retreat in Idaho, he took a double-barreled shotgun and blew his head off. Guilt had filled every room of his being, and he felt his only way out was suicide. His blood-stained body was a brief testimony to the destructiveness of sin.

Marilyn Monroe was the sex queen of Hollywood and the idol of thousands. Outwardly, she gave every evidence of being "queen for a day." However, sin did its destructive work on her spirit. Near the end of her life she bitterly complained, "I am just a piece of meat for everyone to chew on." Taking an overdose of sleeping pills, Marilyn saw to it that no one ever used her again. Was suicide the answer? Certainly not.

Forgiveness

We can deal correctly with our sins by allowing Christ to cover our sins with his own blood. The Bible is explicit:

The death and resurrection of Christ is the only permanent cure for sin. Forgiveness becomes real when we confess our sins to Christ and receive, by faith, his eternal Spirit. The Bible states, "In Him we have redemption through His blood, the forgiveness of our trespasses, according to the riches of His grace" (Eph. 1:7); "The blood of Jesus His Son cleanses us from all sin" (1 John 1:7); "To Him, who loves us, and released us from our sins by His blood" (Rev. 1:5).

The Bible is explicit when it says that we can appropriate this forgiveness when we are willing to confess our sins and yield our lives to Christ who died for us: "The blood of Jesus His Son cleanses us from all sin if we confess our sins, He is faithful and righteous to forgive us our sins and to cleanse us from all unrighteousness" (1 John 1:7,9).

The psalmist wrote from experience: "I acknowledged my sin to Thee, . . . And Thou didst forgive the guilt of my sin" (Ps. 32:5). The victory and assurance of the psalmist can be ours when we come to Jesus in faith.

Janet understands forgiveness. Having had several marriages to fail, Janet had turned to alcohol and a social circuit that allowed her to indulge in her favorite pastime. One night, while lying in bed, guilt began to destroy her soul. It seemed to her that the only way out of her misery was suicide. However, a distant voice from within kept saying that God loved her. Falling to her knees, she confessed her sins and sought God's forgiveness. The Lord met her that night, and she found the strength to live again under God's abiding care. Janet found a way to deal with her sins. Instead of trying to drown them in a bottle, she allowed the Lord Jesus to drown her sins in the depths of his love. How shall we deal with our sins? We must go to Jesus and receive his grace as the answer to our guilt.

5

And God Was with Moses

Exodus 2:15-22

A few years ago Mrs. Nell Johnson, an active member of my church, had a tragedy strike someone very dear to her. She had to make an emergency trip to Columbia, Mississippi. Mrs. Virginia Cowden, who was a pilot and owned a small plane, volunteered to fly Nell to Columbia. On the return trip to Amory they were enjoying a smooth flight on a beautiful day. Then the unexpected happened. Without warning the plane's engine stopped, and Mrs. Cowden was unable to get it started. Unknown to them at the time, the fuel line was clogged. Fortunately, the plane was high enough that Virginia had time to prepare for an emergency landing. Both ladies were aware of the danger, and very little was said as the plane began to descend. Like the professional she is, Mrs. Cowden informed Nell that they would have to make an emergency landing, and she started looking for an open field. As she searched frantically for a place to land, the Golden-Triangle Airport appeared on the horizon. Virginia wondered whether they had enough altitude to reach the field. That descent was an experience they will never forget. With silent prayers going up to God, Virginia maneuvered the plane toward the airfield which had been cleared for them. Tall trees and a barbed-wire fence stood between them and the safety of the runway. Brushing the tops of the trees and missing the fence by inches, the plane hit the ground short of the airstrip, bounced once, then landed quietly and smoothly on the concrete. A pilot's skill and God's grace had brought them safely home.

Like Virginia and Nell, Moses learned that in difficult times God is able to see his people safely home. Although Moses probably felt at times that he had been forsaken, God never abandoned him. For a few moments let us consider how God demonstrated his continuous guidance in the life of Moses by leading him to the land of Midian.

A Place to Live In

God demonstrated his support of Moses by giving him a place in which to live. The Lord led him to the land of Midian. Midian consisted of an area in the northwest Arabian Desert, east of the Gulf of Aqabah, and part of the Sinai Desert. Some scholars think the Midianites entered the Sinai to graze their flocks and to work in the copper mines.[1]

Although the land of Midian in no way compared to the splendor of Egypt, it contained people who were receptive to Moses. Here he put down roots and struggled to know himself and God's will for his life.

Every man needs a place he can call home. While I enjoy taking vacations and visiting relatives, a time comes when I am ready to return home. It is a wonderful feeling to enter into the city limits of my hometown and see familiar buildings and streets. It is even a greater feeling to walk through the door of our home and touch the objects that make our house our home. I have also observed that on returning home, our three-year-old son runs through all the rooms and touches all his toys. He, too, is thrilled to be home. Having a home gives a person a sense of security and makes a person feel as if he belongs. It also gives confidence and hope. Moses needed that sense of security and well-being, and he gradually found it as he spent forty years in Midian.

One of the most moving speeches I have ever heard was given by Henry Kissinger when he made his farewell address, ending his eight years as secretary of state. With tears in his eyes he expressed gratitude for America. To him it had been a place where a German-Jewish immigrant could live and develop his creative talents. His speech reminded me of the importance of having a place where one can feel at home. Like Kissinger, Moses was given a new place to call home. Midian provided him with an opportunity to grow and mature. For Moses it was a new beginning.

People to Live With

God demonstrated his support of Moses by leading him to people with whom he could live. In Midian Moses met and married Zipporah. *Zipporah* means "little bird." If ancient names denote character, Zipporah was either very small or she chattered a lot. Nevertheless, the Lord provided Moses with a wife who could share his thoughts and meet his needs.

Exodus 2:22 and 18:2-5 state that Moses and Zipporah had two sons, Gershom and Eliezer. No doubt, in loving them, Moses came to understand partially God's love for him. The need to love and be loved is basic to all men. Through loving relationship, we grow and mature. The Lord provided the ingredients whereby Moses could love and be loved.

In Midian Moses also gained a father-in-law, Jethro. This man became a trusted friend whose advice was wise and helpful. In Exodus 18 we are told that Moses was having difficulty ministering to the needs of his people as they marched to the Promised Land. Jethro told Moses that he was trying to do too much. He suggested that Moses select, from the people, wise elders who could assist him in the various decisions which had to be made. In response to this suggestion, "Moses listened to his father-in-law, and did all that he had said" (Ex. 18:24). Moses demonstrated maturity when he listened to one older and wiser.

Young people do themselves a favor when they listen with open minds to the advice of their elders. Those who do not listen usually have to pay a high price for their stupidity. In 1 Kings 12:1-15, the Bible states that Rehoboam became king of Israel after the death of his father, Solomon. The people approached the new king and asked for a reduction in taxes. Rehoboam consulted with the elders who advised: "Grant them their petition, and speak good words to them, then they will be your servants forever" (1 Kings 12:7). However, his young advisers suggested he tell the people, "Whereas my father loaded you with a heavy yoke, I will add to your yoke; my father disciplined you with whips, but I will discipline you with scorpions" (1 Kings 12:11). Rehoboam rejected the advice of his elders and lost half of his kingdom. The people rebelled; the kingdom was divided.

In Midian Moses found people whom he could love and trust. This is another example of how God sustained his prophet in those difficult years after his expulsion from Egypt.

A Purpose to Live For

God demonstrated his support of Moses by giving him a purpose for which to live. In Midian, God made Moses into a shepherd. It was quite a contrast to the marble halls of the Egyptian palace; however, it was an experience

Moses needed in preparation for leading the people out of Egypt.

His life as a shepherd was a training ground for the future. At this time Moses learned to cope with the desert, a place where he would lead the Hebrews for forty years. He came to know the rocks, the sands, and the desert winds. He learned the heartbeat of the desert and how to survive its hot days and cold nights. He discovered the water holes and the quicksands and learned that the desert could be a friend if handled correctly.

In this training school Moses learned to sacrifice for his sheep. This prepared him for the time when he would sacrifice for his people. At this time he developed patience. Sheep are helpless creatures which need a patient shepherd. In the years that followed his time in Midian, Moses found his people spending much of their time acting like helpless sheep.

Second, Moses' life as a shepherd was a theological school for spiritual growth. Like the shepherd of Psalm 23, Moses came to the conclusion that the Lord was his shepherd and would provide for all his needs. I have a feeling that when Moses reached this conclusion God appeared to him in the burning bush.

Third, Moses' life as a shepherd was a time of serious thinking. As he wandered alone in the desert, tending his sheep, I believe Moses asked the great questions of life, Who am I? Why am I? Where am I Going? I am confident it was during the time Moses was in the desert, that he came to realize he was a person deeply loved by God. At this time in his life Moses discovered he could be used as a vessel through which God's Spirit could work with power.

Psychiatrist James D. Mallory is correct when he suggests that all men have three very basic needs: to love and be loved; to feel worthwhile to themselves and others; and to have a purpose for living.[2] When Moses was a fugitive from the law, God led him to Midian and met those basic needs. When we trust God, he will meet our needs, just as he met Moses' needs thousands of years ago.

6

God Doesn't Stumble in the Dark

Exodus 2:23-25

Since my wife and I have two small boys, a three-year-old and a one-year-old, we are often up in the middle of the night tending to their needs and making sure they are under the blankets rather than on top of them. On one occasion, at approximately 3:00 AM, I was staggering down a cold, darkened hallway in response to a cry for water. By the time I was awake enough to get the water and to find my way to my older son's room, he had fallen asleep. Having made this futile trip, I attempted to return to my bedroom—a return trip which was almost disaster. In my hurry to return to the warmth of my bed, I had forgotten that my wife had moved the coffee table from the living room to the bedroom. My shins met the immovable object.

As I have reflected on this experience, the thought has come to my mind that God never stumbles in the dark. Man may fall, but God never does. The psalmist was correct when he wrote: "Even the darkness is not dark to Thee,/And the night is as bright as the day./Darkness and light are alike *to Thee*" (Ps. 139:12). In the midst of the confusion and chaos of this world, let us remember that our heavenly Father is still in control of this universe. He is not floundering on the sea of despair. Our great God is able to meet our needs.

God Knows About the Problem

Our problems always seem immense. Most of the time we feel as if we are the only folk who have any serious problems. Man has always responded in this manner. If answers are not received instantaneously from God, we tend to feel that God is totally unaware of us; however, this is not true. Some of the Hebrew people probably felt that God had abandoned them, as the Egyptian persecution increased. But the Bible says, "God heard their groaning" (Ex. 2:24). The Lord was cognizant of their problems. He had already set in motion a plan whereby he would answer their prayers.

The Lord is always aware when we are hurting, and he seeks continually to minister to us. In John 4 the Bible reveals how Jesus confronted a disillusioned woman at Jacob's well. This woman of Samaria had failed at marriage so many times that she had decided love and loyalty were myths to be enjoyed by daydreamers. At the well she met God's Son and discovered that love and loyalty were genuine attributes of a concerned God. After meeting Jesus, she realized God knew about her problems and he had the power to bring healing and forgiveness to a shattered life.

The apostle Peter denied Jesus three times and then fled into the night to weep bitter repentant tears. John 21 states that Jesus confronted Peter and offered hope to a man who had failed. The Lord was aware of the apostle's problems and provided grace for a broken heart. On that day, beside the clear waters of a beautiful lake, Peter discovered that God was cognizant of his needs and could bring healing to a weeping heart.

In John 8 the Word of God introduces us to a woman caught in adultery. Without a doubt, she knew the hurt that sin and guilt can bring to life. Adding to her despair was the hypocrisy of a male society which sought to use her as a pawn. However, she discovered that God knew about her hurting and that he had the power to restore a broken life. Offering her a second chance, Jesus told her to go and sin no more.

Mary and Martha knew real grief (John 11). In the midst of their grief, Jesus came to their home to say that he knew they were heartbroken. He demonstrated to them that he had the power to conquer death.

What is your problem? Are you plagued by sin and guilt? Jesus knows you are hurting, and he offers you his forgiveness. Have you failed? Jesus knows you are downcast, and he offers you his grace and his strength to begin again. Are you lost in the tunnel called grief? Jesus knows you are crying, and he seeks to minister to your sorrow. Offer up your life to the living Christ and allow him to share in your hurt. Do not give up. If you believe you have reached the end of your rope, tie a knot and hang on. God is going to help you.

God Hears Our Pleas

The Scripture text reveals that God hears our pleas and is affected by them. Our prayers do not rise to a stone-faced God who is indifferent to our wounds. Our pleas are sensitive sounds to an all-knowing and merciful God. As the Hebrews confronted pain and persecution and cried out for help, the living Lord was in the very process of unveiling his plan of redemption. Although God may not always act in the way we wish, we can be sure that he is acting within the scope of his divine will and purpose. He hears our pleas and acts according to his divine sovereignty.

Jesus prayed in the garden prior to his death and earnestly asked that he might be delivered from the cross and the burden of bearing man's sin. The heavenly Father heard the plea, but he did not spare his Son from death. Instead, Jesus was empowered to accept the Father's will with supernatural courage. The record of the Scripture contends that even in death Christ was in complete control. A Roman soldier was so overwhelmed by the dignity and courage of Jesus he was heard to say that Jesus was truly God's Son.

In 2 Corinthians 12, the Word of God reveals Paul's plea to be healed of some strange disease. The wise apostle tells us that he heard God say, "My grace is sufficient for you" (2 Cor. 12:9). God was aware of Paul's problem; however, God used the pain to demonstrate to Paul and others that God can use our sufferings for his glory and our good.

In Acts 12 we are informed that the church prayed for Peter to be released from prison. This prayer was according to the will of God. A miracle occurred; Peter was delivered from his enemies. Recently a Southern Baptist missionary to Ethiopia had a similar experience. God does hear our pleas and is able to act according to his divine will.

God Keeps His Promise

During the past year the news media has made much of the campaign promises made by President Carter. Reporters are quick to delineate the promises the president has failed to keep. The text that we are studying days, "God remembered His covenant with Abraham, Isaac, and Jacob" (Ex. 2:24). God had promised Abraham that he would make a great nation out of Abraham's descendants. When the Hebrews struggled under tyranny, they wondered if God would make good on that promise; however, the people of God were reminded that God always keeps every promise.

Consider for a few moments some of the precious promises of God. One is the promise of forgiveness of sin. Isaiah proclaimed: "Come now, and let us reason together,"/Says the LORD,/"Though your sins are as scarlet,/They will be as white as snow;/Though they are red like crimson, They will be like wool" (Isa. 1:18). When we come to Christ by faith, acknowledging that he died for us, we can be confident that the Lord has truly forgiven us for every sin. We can claim this promise because it is a truth proclaimed throughout the Word of God. Zacchaeus, the Philippian jailer, and many other Bible personalities bear witness to this great promise.

God promises peace. The apostle Paul told us not to go to pieces over anything and to pray about everything with the assurance that "The peace of God, which surpasses all comprehension, shall guard your hearts and your minds in Christ Jesus" (Phil. 4:7). Baker James Cauthen, former executive-secretary of the Foreign Mission Board of the Southern Baptist Convention, had a heart attack while preaching in Huntsville, Alabama. In sharing that experience with his friends, he told us that he was overwhelmed by the peace of God in the moments immediately after his heart attack. He said:

I rose to speak. . . . The next thing I knew, I was lying on the floor with a group of church people around me. . . . An amazing sense of peace possessed me. When asked, "How do you feel?" I replied, "Better than I have felt all night". . . . I cannot express adequately my gratitude for the peace and assurance I felt in those moments. Throughout the night the Scripture had rung in my heart: "For whether we live, we live unto the Lord; and whether we die, we die unto the Lord: whether we live therefore, or die, we are the Lord's.'' As I lay there on the floor, I had a feeling that the Lord was in charge and that all would be well according to His will, whatever that might be. . . . The sense of peace never wavered.[1]

The Lord kept his promise to a man who had fulfilled God's requirements.

Our God never stumbles in the dark. He knows when we are hurting, and he seeks to minister to us. In the midst of all your troubles, do not surrender to self-pity and fear. If you believe you have reached the end of your rope, tie a knot and hang on. The Lord is near, and he is going to see you through this difficult time.

In Egypt the Hebrews learned that God knows our problems, hears our pleas, and keeps his promises. We can learn from the Hebrews' experience in Egypt long ago.

7

The Back Side
of the Desert

Exodus 3:1-4

On August 3, 1492, Christopher Columbus departed Palos, Spain, seeking a new sea route to China. Defying traditional thinking that the world was flat, Columbus sailed west with three ships the *Nina,* the *Pinta,* and the *Santa Maria.* After thirty days at sea, the sailors panicked and demanded that Columbus turn back; however, two days later, at 2 AM, October 12, Columbus discovered the Bahama Islands. Although he did not realize it at the time, his discovery of a new land would change the whole course of human history.

As Columbus went to the back side of the world, Moses went to the back side of the desert and made a great discovery about God and man. Let's consider what Moses learned in that desolate desert.

Holy God

As Moses watched over his sheep, God spoke to him from a burning bush: "The angel of the LORD appeared to him in a blazing fire from the midst of a bush" (Ex. 3:2). The time had come for God to reveal himself to Moses. As Moses debated within himself his own worth and the existence of a living God, the Lord appeared to him to vanquish all doubts. The burning bush was the divine signpost pointing to an eternal God.

Through the ages God has made himself known to man.

The prophet Isaiah attended a worship service in the Temple. Out of this experience he wrote, "In the year of King Uzziah's death, I saw the Lord sitting on a throne, lofty and exalted" (Isa. 6:1). The worship experience brought Isaiah face to face with a holy God.

Years ago an Ethiopian was returning home after worshiping in Jerusalem. God revealed himself to that man through Holy Scripture. He was reading from Isaiah 53 and was not sure of its meaning. Philip, a deacon, approached the Ethiopian and explained the meaning of the passage. The Bible states that Philip "opened his mouth, and beginning from this Scripture he preached Jesus to him" (Acts 8:35). Out of that encounter, the Ethiopian discovered God.

Wernher Von Braun, the German scientist who led America into the space age, came to believe in God through his study of the stars. His logical conclusion was that only the existence of God could account for the orderly universe. As this wise man explored the depths of the universe, God revealed himself forcefully and clearly.

At the burning bush, a holy God, who deeply cares for man, was revealed to Moses. As God spoke and revealed his plan to redeem the Hebrews from Egypt, Moses realized that God was not a mere spectator in history but was an active participant in its outcome. The prophet discovered that God is not indifferent to man's needs but that he is a living God, who is ever seeking to enter man's existence to offer assistance. God is never late; he is always exactly on time.

We can meet a holy God just as Moses did. God has not called us to a burning bush, but he has called us to a burning tree that is called the Cross of Christ. Peter reminds us "He [Jesus] Himself bore our sins in His body on the cross, that we might die to sin and live to righteousness; for by His wounds you were healed" (1 Pet. 2:24). The God that Moses knew is the God that we come to know in Jesus Christ. The Cross of Jesus was God's tree set afire by the love of God, revealing to us both our sin and our worth before God. The victory that God proclaimed to Moses at the burning bush is the victory proclaimed to us at the Cross. We have a loving God who is deeply interested in us, a God who desires to dwell in our hearts. By faith we can open our lives to him and receive his love and grace.

Holy Ground

In the back side of the desert, Moses not only discovered a holy God but he also learned that he was standing on holy ground. God said, "Remove your sandals from your feet, for the place on which you are standing is holy ground" (Ex. 3:5).

Various religions have what could be called holy ground. Near the town of Amory, Mississippi, are ancient Indian burial grounds. Even now archeologists are digging into these mounds trying to piece together the life of the ancient Chickasaw Indian nation. To the Indians the burial grounds were holy ground where the spirits of the dead lingered. The land that comprised the burial grounds was sacred and was not to be entered except under specific conditions.

To the Muslims certain areas within the city of Mecca and Jerusalem are considered to be holy ground. Muslims remove their shoes before entering a sacred shrine or temple. They take seriously the concept of holy ground.

I believe that at the burning bush God was telling Moses that all of life is to be viewed as holy ground. This is true because God's people are always in the presence of a holy God. Life is sacred, and God would have us understand that we should live in the awareness that he is always with us. The New Testament reminds us that our bodies are the temple of the Holy Spirit. Every step we take is a step taken in his presence.

It is very difficult to grasp this truth. After Moses died, the Jews wanted to relegate God to a specific place. God's holiness was thought to be revealed at certain places on designated days. Let us not make the same mistake. The apostle Paul stressed the sacredness of living when he said, "Whatever you *do* in word or deed, do all in the name of the Lord Jesus" (Col. 3:17).

The Bible gives us at least two reasons for treating all of life as if it were a walk on holy ground before a holy God. First, we were bought with a price, and we are not our own: "You have been bought with a price: therefore glorify God in your body" (1 Cor. 6:20). Second, we are indwelt by the Holy Spirit. "Do you know that your body is a temple of the Holy Spirit who is in you?" (1 Cor. 6:19). The believer is informed that he not only stands before a holy God but he also has a holy God living in his life. When a man comes to realize that all of life is sacred, drastic and positive changes will be made in his school life, business life, dating life, social life, and in every other activity that constitutes his walk as a believer. Like Moses he will learn that he is continuously in the presence of a holy God who requires that he treat all of life as holy ground.

Holy Grace

At the burning bush Moses realized that he was the recipient of holy grace. Why did God choose Moses to be the deliverer of his people? Certainly Moses' past life did not merit God's favor. His adopted homeland, Midian, was not a nation of great worth. Since he was living off his father-in-law, Moses had no special financial status. God did not choose Moses because of anything that Moses had accomplished; the choice was rooted in God's grace. God's character made Moses a great leader, and everything that Moses was able to do came about because of God's grace.

Moses was chosen by God's grace. God reaches out and saves us, not because of who we are but because of who he is—a God of grace. He is love and that love compels him to reach out to us. Long before we ever give God a thought, God has his eyes on us. The apostle Paul put it best when he wrote: "For by grace you have been saved through faith; and that not of yourselves, *it is* the gift of God" (Eph. 2:8). *Grace* is difficult for us to comprehend because in human relationships we emphasize *merit*. A student receives a scholarship because of his outstanding grades. The scholarship is something he deserved. A businessman receives an expense-paid trip to Paris because he was the leading salesman for his company. He received the honor he merited. The football player receives a million-dollar contract because of his superior ability. The young lady is crowned Miss America because of her beauty and talent. Examples of merit are endless; however, our relationship to God is established in God's character, not on our accomplishments.

Before Evangelist Gypsy Smith was converted, he made a living carving clothespins. Eventually, he became an internationally known minister, who was entertained by kings and heads of state. In his home, in a place of prominence, he kept the old knife that he had used to carve clothespins. When he began to feel proud, the knife reminded him of what he had been before God touched him with heavenly grace.

Moses knelt before a burning bush and discovered that there is a holy God, that he was standing on holy ground, and that he was the recipient of holy grace. May we learn these simple truths for victorious living!

8

The Revealing God

Exodus 3:2-4

Where and how does God reveal himself? Tradition has programmed us to believe that God reveals himself to people in worship. Certainly the experience of the prophet Isaiah, as recorded in Isaiah 6, confirms the truth that God often reveals himself in times of worship. God also reveals himself in other ways. He reveals himself in nature. The psalmist cried, "The heavens are telling of the glory of God;/And their expanse is declaring the work of His hands" (Ps. 19:1). God reveals himself in Scripture. In Acts 8 we are informed that an Ethiopian was reading from Isaiah 53. Philip, a deacon, shared with the Ethiopian that Jesus Christ is the fulfillment of that prophecy in Isaiah. Out of that experience the Ethopian was converted. God reveals himself in prayer. Second Corinthians 12 tells of Paul's struggle with a physical problem and how he asked God for healing. God did not heal the disease; however, Paul did hear God say, "My grace is sufficient for you, for power is perfected in weakness" (2 Cor. 12:9).

God revealed himself to Moses in a burning bush: "The angel of the LORD appeared to him in a blazing fire from the midst of a bush; and he looked, and behold, the bush was burning with fire, yet the bush was not consumed" (Ex. 3:2). From this experience in the life of Moses, let us observe how God reveals himself in unusual places, at unexpected times, and in uncommon circumstances.

Unusual Places

God reveals himself in unusual places. For Moses the revelation was in the desert. There were no churches, Sunday Schools, Bibles, or revival meetings in the immediate area. Moses did not have the benefit of a seminary or a religious conference on the deeper life. In the desert there were just rocks, hot sands, dirty sheep, shifting winds, and a bush. That was all God needed because he is in the business of revealing himself where men least expect it.

The apostle John received a revelation from God while in exile on the island of Patmos:

After these things I looked, and behold, a door *standing* open in heaven, and the first voice which I had heard, like *the sound* of a trumpet speaking with me, said, "Come up here, and I will show you what must take place after these things." Immediately I was in the Spirit; and behold, a throne was standing in heaven, and One sitting on the throne (Rev. 4:1-2).

From exile, a most unusual place for inspiration, John received a message that has continued to give hope to Christians down through the ages.

Who would have thought that God would reveal himself in a desert or on an island? The fact that he did simply demonstrates that one can never limit God, who is in the business of speaking from unusual places.

Anita Bryant almost died giving birth to twins on January 1, 1969. Soon after the births, Anita and her husband, Bob Green, were informed that the twins would probably die. At first Anita refused to believe that God would allow her babies to die. Through the help of their pastor, Anita and Bob came to understand that their babies might die and, with a prayer of faith, relinquished the twins into God's hands. In the same hour the Greens said they wanted God's will to be fulfilled, the babies made a turn for the better. For Anita and Bob it was the beginning of a new spiritual growth with the Lord. In the maternity ward of a hospital in Miami, Florida, God revealed himself to the Green family. Indeed, it was a most unusual place.[1]

The experiences of Moses, John, and Mr. and Mrs. Bob Green remind us that God is in the business of revealing himself in unuusual places.

Unexpected Times

Not only does God reveal himself in unusual places but he also reveals himself at unexpected times. I suppose at this time Moses felt like he was a nobody. He had lost all his wealth and status and was living off the bounty of his father-in-law. Without a doubt it was a low time for Moses. The last person he expected to meet was a God with a great commission.

The Scriptures inform us that the apostle Paul met the living Christ while enroute to persecute Christians. "It came about that as he journeyed, he was approaching Damascus, and suddenly a light from heaven flashed around him; and he fell to the ground, and heard a voice saying to him, 'Saul, Saul, why are you persecuting Me?' " (Acts 9:3-4). What an unexpected time to meet God! Who would have thought that God would give a man like Paul the opportunity to be save? Once again we are reminded that God reveals himself at unexpected times.

In the Gospel of John we are introduced to a woman who was living the life of a harlot. She had given up on morals and marriage and was content to drift in a mean-ingless existence. Going to the well in Samaria to draw water, as she had done hundreds of times, she met the living God, Jesus. She left her bucket at the well, but she returned home with a heart filled with God's love. She was so excited, and her testimony was so powerful, that it was said: "From that city many of the Samaritans believed in Him because of the word of the woman who testified, 'He told me all the things that I *have* done' " (John 4:39). Yes, God does reveal himself at unexpected times.

In April, 1964, Ann McGee of Birmingham, Alabama, was severely injured in an automobile accident. In this accident her husband was killed and her son seriously injured. The doctors had to literally wire her body back together, and she spent almost a year in the hospital. While in a deep depression, she was visited by her doctor, who gave her a slip of paper. On the paper was written: "Truly I say to you, whoever says to this mountain, 'Be taken up and cast into the sea, and does not doubt in his heart, but believes that what he says is going to happen, it shall be *granted* him" (Mark 11:23). In that moment God revealed himself anew to Ann McGee. In reflecting on that unexpected time when God spoke to her heart, Ann said: "People have asked me if I had ever doubted God after the accident. I haven't . . . . There have been times I have wanted to work things out my own way; but when I leave problems in God's hands, they always work out. That verse that I carried with me through surgery—and I still carry it—makes me remember that God is close by.[2] Yes, God does reveal himself at unexpected times.

Uncommon Circumstances

God is able to use uncommon circumstances in which to reveal his presence. For Moses it was a burning bush. One does not normally expect to find a bush that is burning and yet is not consumed. Imagine Moses' surprise when he learned that God was speaking from the burning bush!

God's prophet, Hosea, came to understand through a very tragic circumstance the love of God for a rebellious people. Like any normal young man, Hosea fell in love and married the girl of his heart. Three children were born to this union. Suddenly the unexpected happened. Gomer, Hosea's wife, deserted him and began living as a common prostitute. It is not known exactly why she did this. She probably got caught up in the spirit of the times. Permissiveness was accepted and practiced with regularity. Hosea lived with the innuendoes and malicious gossip of his neighbors. One day, as he walked through the market place, he was astonished to find Gomer on the slave block being auctioned off to the highest bidder. All her paramours had finally rejected her, and she now stood naked for all to see. Gazing at her abused body, Hosea again felt the rivers of love flowing through his heart. As tears filled his eyes he heard God speak:

"Go again, love a woman *who* is loved by *her* husband, yet an adulteress, even as the Lord loves the sons of Israel, though they turn to other gods and love raisin cakes." So I bought her for myeslf for fifteen *shekels* of silver and a homer and a half of barley (Hos. 3:1-2).

The crowd stepped back, allowing Hosea to approach the slave block. As he moved through the sea of a thousand eyes, he could hear the whispers of contempt and the sarcastic laughter. Hosea softly told the auctioneer that he wanted this slave. After paying for Gomer, Hosea looked directly into her face. The years of meaningless living had taken their toll; and it was difficult to realize that she had at one time been beautiful. After removing his coat, he wrapped it around her body. Putting one arm around her shoulders and gently taking her hand, Hosea led Gomer off the slave block and through the crowd. The crowd was silent, astonished at what they were witnessing. As Hosea walked home with Gomer, he began to understand how God must feel when his own people rejected him. This experience had given Hosea a new vision of the love of God. Out of this tragic circumstance, God had prepared Hosea to be a great witness of God's love.

All of these revelations remind us that no one is far from God. God is not limited by deserts, islands accidents, or disappointments. He can turn unusual places, unexpected times, and uncommon circumstances into broad highways of divine revelation. When we least expect him, God comes to us in all his glory!

9

The Inflammables

Exodus 3:2; Matthew 13:42; Luke 24:32

During our days at New Orleans Baptist Theological Seminary, my wife and I lived by a very busy schedule. She was a part-time secretary for one of the professors and attended college classes in the afternoon. I attended seminary classes in the morning, taught school in the afternoon, and pastored a small, country church on the weekend. One afternoon I arrived earlier than usual at our seminary apartment. Marty was still in class, and I decided that I would be the good Samaritan and prepare our dinner.

I had never cooked chicken; however I had watched my wife frying the fowl on numerous occasions and was quite sure that I could do the same. My deduction proved to be wrong. I poured the grease into the frying pan and allowed it to get too hot. When I dropped the first piece of chicken into the hot grease, it caught fire, and flames shot up to the ceiling. Instead of covering the fire with the lid of the pan, I panicked and did what one should never do—I threw cold water on the hot grease. The water only intensified the fire and filled the apartment with smoke. As the smoke poured out of the window of our third-floor apartment, students living below us thought the building was on fire and called the fire department. If God had spoken to me from that burning grease, as he spoke to Moses from a burning bush, I am quite sure I would have fainted.

The Bible speaks of a burning bush, a burning hell, and a burning heart:

"He looked, and behold, the bush was burning with fire, yet the bush was not consumed" (Ex. 3:2); "The Son of Man will send forth His angels . . . and will cast them into the furnace of fire" (Matt. 13:41-42); "And they said to one another, 'Were not our hearts burning within us while He was speaking to us on the road?' " (Luke 24:32).

God's Realness

The burning bush speaks of God's realness. It tells us that God's initiative in seeking man is real. At the burning bush Moses met a living God, who was in the business of reaching people. God was not simply sitting on his throne, apathetically viewing man's suffering. He is a God who reaches out to heal the bruised hearts and minds of folks who experience the worst the world could offer.

The burning bush of Moses' experience tells us that God's love is real. God does not love in the abstract. He wants his love to be felt and experienced. Moses left the burning bush with authority and power to demonstrate to the Hebrews that God's love is genuine. God would move through his prophet, confirming that he had come to embrace his people in his eternal arms.

God loves us because he is God and we are persons created in his image. This truth is not always easy to accept. The Lord loves us because we are persons, not because of our accomplishments. While viewing a therapy session at a state institution, Harold G. Warlick, Jr., heard the therapist ask a patient, "Why do people like you?"

The patient responded, "Because I have a beautiful home. I provide for my family. I have excelled in my various pursuits."

The therapist inquired, "Do you have any feelings of being loved simply for yourself and not for the things your skills have generated?" The patient was silent and began to cry.[1]

Man does find it difficult to believe that God loves because man is created in the image of God. God's love is not based on what a man has accomplished. Let us go to the burning bush and discover the real God who loves us just as he loved Moses and the Hebrew people.

God's Rejection

The burning hell speaks of God's rejection. In the revelation to Moses, God warned that he would judge Egypt: "So I will stretch out My hand, and strike Egypt with all My miracles which I shall do in the midst of it" (Ex. 3:20). Because Egypt would reject God's authority, God would smite Egypt. At the burning bush Moses confronted God's realness, but he also heard of God's rejection. In the New Testament this rejection is explained in terms of hell. Jesus said, "The Son of Man will send forth His angels, and they will gather out of His kingdom all STUMBLING BLOCKS, AND THOSE WHO COMMIT LAWLESSNESS, and will cast them into the furnace of fire; in that place there shall be weeping and gnashing of teeth" (Matt. 13: 41-42).

God's love and God's hell is the paradox of Jesus. The Lord spoke of God's love and demonstrated it completely in his own life. He was also the one who emphatically proclaimed the reality of hell.

How shall we treat this subject? Some have simply said there is no God; therefore, there is no hell. A few men have proclaimed that God is real but have contended that *hell* is only a psychological term to describe a meaningless existence. A few men have even suggested that God's love is so great he will save all men; therefore, hell is really a myth. The New Testament seems to say that hell is real and those who reject God on this side of eternity have reserved for themselves a permanent residence in its eternal flames.

Jesus said, "So it will be at the end of the age; the angels shall come forth, and take out the wicked from among the righteous, and will cast them into the furnace of fire; there shall be weeping and gnashing of teeth" (Matt. 13:49-50).

Jesus told a parable concerning the rich man and Lazarus. The devastating parable proclaims an eternal judgment. Jesus has the rich man crying, "Have mercy on me, and send Lazarus, that he may dip the tip of his finger in water and cool off my tongue; for I am in agony in this flame" (Luke 16:24). I have often wondered what expression was on the face of Jesus when he told this parable. What was the tone of his voice? Were there tears in his eyes?

Although there is much we do not understand about hell, we know enough to realize that it will be a garbage dump for wasted lives. God warned Moses that he would judge Egypt, and he did. God has warned us of an eternal hell. It does exist.

God's Redemption

The burning heart speaks of God's redemption. In Luke 24:32 we read: "And they said to one another, 'Were not our hearts burning within us while He was speaking to us on the road, while He was explaining the Scriptures to us?' " Two disciples, on the road to Emmaus, met the risen Christ. Out of that experience these men knew that Jesus had truly redeemed them from the bondage of sin and death. As they remembered talking with the living Christ, they recalled how their hearts had burned with joy. It was a moment they never forgot.

I have a feeling that Moses had a similar experience at

the burning bush. As he was confronted with God's realness and God's rejection, he was also confronted with God's redemptive power. God said to Moses: "I have surely seen the affliction of My people. . . . So I have come down to deliver them from the power of the Egyptians" (Ex. 3:7-8). The heart of Moses must have burned with joy, knowing that God would redeem his people.

Jeremiah, Zaccheus, Peter, and hundreds of other Bible personalities gave their testimonies of how the living God made their hearts burn with joy because of his redemptive love. Moses met God at the bush; Jeremiah met him at the potter's wheel; Zaccheus climbed down from a tree and found him; Peter encountered him at the seashore. Although the places were different, the message was the same: God can set his people free from sin's destructiveness. The living God of Israel is in the business of redeeming people.

Grandma Minnie Neadercook Tucker was born around 1860 in Alaska. At that time the land was still owned by the Russians. Her Eskimo parents were good people who taught her to respect life and to love others. Minnie had eight children, all of whom she delivered herself. In her lifetime she delivered many babies. She said, "My hands are always warm. Babies like my hands. The mammas do, too."

After her husband's death, Minnie moved to Fairbanks, Alaska. One day she told a friend: "I want to see real preachers preaching. I want to go to church." Minnie did go to church, and eventually she accepted Christ. Being illiterate, Minnie told a friend she wanted to learn to read and write. She said, "I really want to learn Jesus' name. I want to learn the important name and that is Jesus, not Minnie." A missionary taught her to write the name of Jesus. One day the missionary visited Minnie and discovered that she had printed the name *Jesus* on the cracker box, a calendar, paper bags, and on other items in the room. Minnie learned to find the name *Jesus* in the Bible. One time friends discovered her newspaper had twenty-two lines drawn on it. She exclaimed. "That is how many times I found Jesus' name. He is all through the Bible."

Grandma Minnie Tucker was saved when she was nearly 100 years old and learned to read at 106. She died and went to heaven at 117 years of age. She experienced completely God's redemptive power, and so can you.

10

God Knows Your Name

Exodus 3:4

The Bible says that, as Moses approached the burning bush, "God called to him from the midst of the bush, and said, 'Moses, Moses!' And he said, 'Here I am' " (Ex. 3:4). This was a great moment in the life of Moses. He realized that God knew him by name.

My three-year-old son is named Jon Stephen Kennedy. We call him Steve. Occasionally, when he is asked for his name, he says, "Roy Desoto." Now, for you who are not on to TV, Roy Desoto is one of the leading characters on the program *Emergency.* My son is very partial to firemen. The other day he was asked his name, and he gave his typical reply, "Roy Desoto." Being a little disturbed by his unwillingness to give his proper name, I gave him a stern look and in a very serious voice told him to give his correct name. He dropped his head and without looking up, he replied, "Jon Stephen Kennedy Roy Desoto." I am glad to know that the Lord and I know his real name, even if he refuses to acknowledge it.

The ability to remember names is a wonderful gift. Jim Farley, chairman of the Democratic National Committee and Postmaster General of the United States during the administration of Franklin D. Roosevelt, was a man who possessed this gift. A reporter once asked Farley if it were true that he could call ten thousand people by name. He said, "No. You are wrong. I can call fifty-thousand people by their first names."[1] No doubt Farley's positive personality and his ability to remember names were instrumental in getting Roosevelt elected to the highest office in the land.

When Mamie Eisenhower was first lady at the White House, over seventy servants were employed to keep the presidential home at top efficiency. Mamie could call all of the White House employees by name, and she always baked cakes for their birthdays. About the only time she was not mingling with the servants was at the noon hour when she was in her bedroom watching the TV program *As the World Turns.* Her ability to remember names and mix freely with folk made her a popular first lady.

Although Jim Farley and Mamie Eisenhower excelled in remembering names, their abilities were limited when compared to the Lord. There are over four billion people on this planet, speaking at least twenty-eight hundred different languages and dialects; God knows every one by name. Every man considers his name to be important. We appreciate those who remember our names. Just think, God knows every name on this earth!

God knows your name. Consider with me three reasons why we know God knows our names and what it means for us.

Discerns Our Names

God discerns our names. When God revealed himself to Moses, he did not say, "Hey, you!" or "Hey, Boy!" When my older son was learning to talk, he would call to a stranger, "Hey, Man!" If he saw a blonde woman, he said, "Hey, Mama." However, the Lord was precise when he called, "Moses, Moses!"

The Bible is filled with illustrations of how God called people by name. In 1 Samuel 3, the Bible tells us how God called young Samuel to be a prophet. As he was sleeping near the old priest, Eli, Samuel sensed that God was calling him. When he shared this fact with Eli, the priest suggested that the next time Samuel heard the voice he should say, "Speak, LORD, for Thy servant is listening" (1 Sam. 3:9). Again the voice of God came. The Bible says: "Then the LORD came and stood and called as at other times, 'Samuel, Samuel!' " (1 Sam. 3:10). It was a great moment in the life of the young man when he realized that God knew his name.

As Jesus called his disciples, they were all quick to share with their friends the belief that they had found the Messiah. Philip was so excited he insisted that Nathanael meet Jesus. Reluctantly, Nathanael followed Philip. Upon seeing Jesus, Nathanael heard the Lord say that he (Nathanael) was a man empty of all guile. Nathanael asked, " 'How do You know me?' Jesus answered and said to him, 'Before Philip called you, when you were under the fig tree, I saw you' " (John 1:48). What a thrill for Nathanael to realize that Jesus knew him so intimately!

One day a tax collector wanted to get a view of Jesus. Because he was a small man, he climbed a tree for a better view. To his surprise Jesus walked under the tree, looked up, and said, "Zaccheus, hurry and come down, for today I must stay at your house" (Luke 19:5). Can you imagine the shock Zaccheus felt? He was the most despised man in town. Who would have guessed that Jesus would know his name? Jesus knows every man's name!

With blood in his eyes and hate in his heart, Saul had but one purpose: to destroy the followers of Christ. In the middle of his quest, he heard Jesus say, "Saul, Saul, why are you persecuting Me?" (Acts 9:4). Yes, the Lord even knew Saul's name!

When the Bible reminds us that God discerns our

names, the Spirit of God is telling us that God knows us as
persons. To the Hebrews a man's name and his personality were inseparable. God's ability to call our names
stresses the truth that God is deeply interested in us as
persons. Jesus said, "Are not two sparrows sold for a
cent? And *yet* not one of them will fall to the ground apart
from your Father. But the very hairs of your head are all
numbered. Therefore do not fear; you are of more value
than many sparrows" (Matt. 10:29-31).

When God called Moses, Samuel, Nathanael, Zaccheus,
and Saul, he was calling them into his love. They discovered that the God who knew them by name is the Lord of
glory who wanted to share his presence with them.
Through their various encounters with God, they learned
of their self-worth and how they were important to God as
persons.

As a child I loved to play outside. In the evenings my
mother would come to the back door and call my name,
reminding me that dinner was ready and that it was time to
come home. Today I remember those moments with great
joy. My mother called my name; she wanted me in her
protection and presence. As God calls us by name, he, too,
is calling us into his protection and presence.

Died for Our Names

The Scriptures reminds us that Jesus Christ died for us:
"God demonstrates His own love toward us, in that while
we were yet sinners, Christ died for us" (Rom. 5:8); "I
delivered to you as of first importance what I also received, that Christ died for our sins according to the Scriptures" (1 Cor. 15:3).

Remembering that to the Hebrews a man's name and
his personality were inseparable, I know the above Scriptures proclaim the fact that Jesus died for "Larry Ken-

nedy." When reading the above Scriptures, remove the personal pronouns and insert your own name. This forces home the truth that Jesus did not simply die for mankind, he died for you. He had your name in his heart when he went to the Cross.

A minister, whom I have met numerous times, can never recall my name. When we meet he always calls me by a name other than my own. I believe that man is so preoccupied with himself that he continually looks right through people and never sees them as individuals. How thankful we are that God is not that way. He is not preoccupied with himself. His mind is centered on you and me. He knows our names and calls to us as individuals. He died for us that we might know his name—Jesus, Lord, and Savior. In those moments when you are tempted to doubt your self-worth and importance to God, always remember that the Lord can call you by name and that it was for you he died.

Desires to Write Our Names

When God called Moses by name, he had also written Moses' name in his book. Figuratively speaking, there is a book in heaven that contains the names of those who belong to God. Paul wrote: "Indeed, true comrade, I ask you also to help these women . . . and the rest of my fellow-workers, whose names are in the book of life" (Phil. 4:3). John wrote: "And I saw the dead, the great and the small, standing before the throne, and books were opened; and another book was opened, which is *the book* of life; and the dead were judged from the things which were written in the books, according to their deeds" (Rev. 20:12). Moses, Samuel, Nathanael, Zaccheus, and Paul have their names inscribed in the book of life.

God discerns our names, and he died for our names—

for us. When we respond in faith to God's call and his Cross, the Lord writes our names in his book. He reserves for us a place in his eternal kingdom.

There are some books that I do not care to have my name written in. I would not be excited about seeing my name on the FBI list of the ten, most-wanted men. At the moment I am really not excited about seeing my name in the local obituary column. The telephone company is always wanting to put my name in bold black letters in the telephone book. I refuse—every hobo who comes through town at midnight would be calling me. However, I do want my name in God's book because it means that my "person" will also be in heaven one day.

My father is retired from civil service and now works part-time as a doorman at a penthouse. The only way a stranger can get into that place is by having his name pre-registered at the front desk by a permanent occupant of the penthouse. If the stranger's name is not in the ledger, he does not get in. Only those who have their names in God's book will be allowed in God's heaven. You can have your name inscribed in that book when, by faith, you receive Jesus Christ into your heart. God is calling you by name. Respond to God's call and allow him to write your name in the book of life. I can assure you that you will not regret this decision. Yes, God discerns our names, he died for our names, and he desires to write our names in the book of life.

11
Ever Been Afraid?

Exodus 3:6

Concerning Moses' encounter with God at the burning bush, the Bible states that "Moses hid his face, for he was afraid to look at God" (Ex. 3:6). Moses experienced genuine fear. Have you ever been afraid?

I have known real fear. One childhood experience I remember was when a friend and I were playing in a strange neighborhood. We had no business being there. We spotted other children playing in a backyard and decided to join them. Between us and the children was a huge black dog chained to a tree. Although we did not realize it at the time, this dog was used as a guard at Richie's Liquor Store. We studied the situation carefully and concluded that the chain was short and that, if we ran quickly, we could get past the dog. My courageous friend decided to go first. As he rushed through the yard, the dog jumped at him with a vicious growl, but the chain prevented the dog from reaching my friend. Once on the other side, he motioned to me to make the dash. Confident that I could do the same, I started running across the yard. Halfway across the yard I got too close to the dog, and he pounced upon my back. As the dog growled and chewed at my back, I used all my strength to crawl out of his reach. Fortunately for me, the dog's chain held; and I was able to crawl free. Instantly I remembered my mother telling me never to go near bad dogs because if bitten I could contract rabies. Fear gripped my heart, and I ran home as fast as my legs would take me. I told my mother what had happened. My mother rushed to the yard where the dog was chained. We learned from neighbors that the dog was free of rabies. To this day, I have a fear of dogs.

In 1967, I spent two weeks in South Africa preaching in a British Baptist church. While there I made many new friends and met many wonderful people. I will never forget one man because of a story he told me. He was a new Christian who had been won to Christ while in a hospital recovering from a nervous breakdown. His mental collapse occurred while he was working in one of the gold mines near Johannesburg. He and several other miners were coming up out of a mine shaft in an elevator when all at once the elevator cable broke. The elevator fell more than a hundred feet, killing his friends and severely injuring him. His most serious injury was mental. As the elevator fell, fear filled every fiber of his being; when the elevator stopped, he was in shock. Even as he relived his ordeal, I could see the old fear in his eyes. Because of the love of many Christians, he had found his way out of a dark abyss; however, he was a man who had known real fear.

Moses Was Afraid

At the burning bush, Moses was afraid. Why did fear grip his heart? I think Moses experienced fear because he was facing the unknown. When we encounter the unknown, we usually experience fear. It is not every day we find a burning bush that is not consumed by the flames and hear God speak from it.

I remember, as a child, going into the operating room for my first surgery. As the nurse rolled me down the corridor of the hopsital to the operating room, my father walked beside me holding my hand. I was afraid, and he understood. I had never been in an operating room. For me it was the unknown.

In reflecting on the fear of the unknown, I am reminded of the young boy who occasionally had to go to the barn at night to get firewood. As he stood at the back door, looking toward the barn, the dark shadows played tricks on his mind. He imagined he saw figures. To secure the firewood, he rushed to the barn and returned as quickly as possible. The darkness was the unknown, and he was afraid.

Moses may have been afraid because he had a misconception of God. Many people fear God because they see God as a tyrant who is out to destroy them. Did Moses believe that God was a tyrant seeking to devour him? Our backgrounds certainly affect our understanding of God. You may have heard the story of a teacher who asked her class what God was like. Receiving no response from the pupils, she picked up a ruler and began hitting the children on the head shouting, "God is love, God is love."

Maybe Moses was afraid because he thought death was near. Death is the unknown; we do not experience death three times a week. Man naturally has moments of fear concerning death. All of us desire to go to heaven, but no one is ready to go right now.

As one preacher expounded on the joys of heaven, he said to the congregation, "All of you who want to go to heaven, raise your hands." Everyone in the congregation raised his hand, except one small man who was sitting in the front pew. The pastor peered over at him and asked, sternly, "Man, don't you want to go to heaven when you die?"

The little man responded, "Oh, uh, yes, but I thought you were trying to get a crowd to go now!"

Is it possible that Moses was afraid because of sin and guilt in his life? Moses had committed murder, and that tragedy probably continued to haunt him. Guilt is the cancer of the soul that produces a tidal wave of fear. When Adam and Eve sinned, they hid from God. The natural consequence of their sin and guilt was fear. This is true for all of us.

I think there is a fifth reason for Moses' fear: He was alone. When the Vietcong captured an American pilot, they kept him apart from other captured American pilots. The Vietcong knew that isolation creates fear; fear was used to break the spirit of the American pilots.

Moses Learned Not to Fear

While Moses experienced fear at the burning bush, he eventually learned that God was his salvation; he did not have to fear anything. The psalmist who shouted, "The Lord is my light and my salvation;/Whom shall I fear?/The Lord is the defense of my life;/Whom shall I dread?/Though a host encamp against me,/My heart will not fear" (Ps. 27:1,3). Moses discovered that God is not someone we need to hide *from;* he is someone we can hide *in.* Like the psalmist, he could say, "Thou art my hiding place" (Ps. 32:7).

The Bible says that "The fear of the Lord is the beginning of wisdom" (Ps. 111:10). The Hebrew word translated "fear" is much closer to our word *reverence.* Here is the paradox: When we fear (reverence) God, he gives us the courage to conquer our daily fears. Certainly, Moses learned that great truth.

We must learn to conquer fear because it is such a destructive force. One day Mr. Plague told Mr. Pilgrim that he was going to Baghdad to kill five thousand people. The next day Mr. Pilgrim informed Mr. Plague that he had killed fifty thousand people. Mr. Plague responded, "No, I only killed five thousand. The others died of fear."

You may have heard the story of the man who accidentally trapped himself inside a refrigerated railroad car. He panicked and began pounding on the door, screaming for help. He just knew that he was going to die; he slumped into a corner and scribbled his last thoughts on the wall. When the railroad car door was opened, the man was found dead. The amazing thing was that the refrigeration system was not working—there was plenty of oxygen in the railroad car. The man did not die of cold. Neither did he die of suffocation. He died from fear!

A Sunday School teacher asked her class members what they feared most. Their responses were revealing: "Not rearing my child correctly," "dying," "having cancer," "being attacked by dogs," "talking before others," "losing my family," "losing my job," "being unloved by God." How thankful we are that God in his wisdom enables us to conquer all our fears. On that first Easter, Jesus came from the tomb and told Mary not to fear. That same Jesus lives today, and he is telling us not to fear for he is with us.

A certain child was always afraid of riding through tunnels. Much to the surprise of her parents she overcame the fear by herself. When her mother asked her why she was no longer afraid, the child responded, "Because I now realize that there is light at both ends." Yes, there is light at both ends of the tunnel of life. That light is the Lord. Don't be afraid!

12
Things in Common

Exodus 3:7-8

What do Henry Kissinger, Phyllis Diller, and Moses have in common with you and me? Have you ever taken a perceptive look at Henry Kissinger? He is short and very stout. His hair is cut very close to his head, and he is always wearing dark-rimmed glasses and a dark suit. His voice is very deep, and he speaks in a monotone. He gives the appearance of being a great scholar. Being a man of keen intellect, he knows how to relate to the great leaders of our world. Now consider Phyllis Diller. She looks like an accident going somewhere to happen. Her hair always appears to have been pressed recently by a hot iron. If you were to meet her in the dark, you would probably have a cardiac arrest. On the surface these two people are as different as night and day; however, they have one thing in common: the need to love and to be loved. They have the same need Moses had. From the ditchdigger in China to the taxicab driver in New York City, all of us share this basic need—to love and be loved.

When God appeared to Moses he said,

"I have surely seen the affliction of My people who are in Egypt, and have given heed to their cry because of their taskmasters, for I am aware of their sufferings. So I have come down to deliver them from the power of the Egyptians, and to bring them up from that land to a good and

spacious land, to a land flowing with milk and honey"
(Ex. 3:7-8).

For Moses and the people of God, this statement was the
beginning of an adventure in which God would begin to
meet their great need to love and be loved. However, from
this man's experience we shall discover that God is also
willing to meet that need in our lives.

The Fact of That Need

The need to love and be loved is basic to all men. A little
girl was sitting on the floor playing with her doll. After a
time, she put the doll down and crawled into her mother's
lap. Her mother asked what was wrong. The child replied,
"I enjoy loving my doll; but, Mother, my doll never loves
me back." I think God has so structured us that we only
find ultimate meaning when we are able to love and be
loved.

If man is going to be able to cope with life, he must have
this basic need met. When this need for love is not met,
men resort to strange, and sometimes harmful, behavior.
The state of Utah executed Gary Gilmore for mass murder. During the trial Gilmore informed the world that he
wanted to die. Several of the psychologists who interviewed him said that he was being truthful when he an-
nounced his desire to be executed. They contended that the
attention from the media made him feel important. TV
cameras took his picture, newspapers plastered his face
across the front page, and his name was heard hourly on
the radio. In a weird sort of way, for Gilmore, this was
love. It was an unrealistic attempt to meet that great need
in his life for love.

As a child, Gilmore was abused. He grew up believing
"I'm not OK." This caused him to look at others and say,

"You're not OK either." Even in killing he was probably trying to fulfill this need for love. Killing a person made him feel important. It was a way of getting the attention of others. His experience reminds us that when this great need for love is not met, the devil can enter in and create a twisted and sick mind.

When I was a sophomore in college, I wrote a paper on the 21 American prisoners of war who decided to remain in China rather than return home at the end of the Korean conflict. As I recall, the group was about evenly divided between white and black. Their IQ's ranged from 95 to 145. The men were from all sections of the United States. A few had been reared in poverty; some were from very wealthy backgrounds. Most of them were simply middle-class folk. However, almost all of them had one thing in common: They were from broken homes. Could it be that these men were easily brainwashed because the great need for love had never been met in their personal lives?

Years ago Hollywood did a movie on a P.O.W. who cracked under the interrogation of the enemy. In probing the young man's background, his captors discovered that he felt his father had never loved him. The boy's father had been a stern military man who did not believe in open displays of affection. The demanding, unyielding father had reared a disturbed young man. Once the enemy exposed his emptiness, the young man became like putty in their hands.

Gilmore and the P.O.W.'s remind us that when the great need for love is not met, men find it difficult to cope with life.

When the need for love is fulfilled, man can cope with almost anything. One of the great stories of our time is of Corrie ten Boom. Because her family protected Jews in Holland during World War II, the ten Boom family was subject to harsh treatment by the Nazis. Corrie and her sister were sent to a concentration camp, but their story was one of victory. Ministering to those around them, they were able to bring the light of God into the depths of hell. Because of the great love they had experienced within their family and their abiding faith in God's love, they were able to cope where others gave in to despair. Corrie's sister died in the camp. Corrie ten Boom was spared and continues to give witness to God's love.

Much has been written about the men who survived the prisoner of war camps in Vietnam. One common denominator continues to appear. Those who made it through the ordeal knew they were loved by their families and by God. The constant realization that someone beyond their cells loved them gave them the courage to live.

Love is a powerful force. When a man walks within its walls, he finds the courage and strength to conquer almost anything.

Fulfilling That Need

The need to love and to be loved can be fulfilled at three levels: a loving God, a loving family, and loving friends. A person can probably make it in life when only one level is being met; however, when one is loved at all three levels, he experiences life at its highest and best.

I cannot determine how your family treats you. I can say, with assurance, that you are deeply loved by God. The Bible proclaims "God is love" (1 John 4:8). The Scriptures go farther and say, "In this is love, not that we loved God, but that He loved us and sent His son *to be* the propitiation [mercy seat] for our sins" (1 John 4:10).

The parables of Luke 15 stress God's love for us. When

Jesus was asked why he associated with sinners, he answered with these beautiful parables. He described a shepherd searching for a lost sheep, reminding us that God is the heavenly shepherd who is always seeking us. He told of a father receiving a rebellious son, who had wasted his life in sinful living. This was his way of reminding us that God loves us even though we are sinners.

Years ago an ancient sailor sought to measure the depths of an uncharted sea. Each time he threw out the line he was unable to touch the bottom of the ocean. With every cast of the line, he would write in his depth chart: "It is deeper than that." We can say that of God's love: It is deeper than we can ever comprehend. "For God so loved the world, that He gave His only begotten Son, that whoever believes in Him should not perish, but have eternal life" (John 3:16).

The Function of God's People

The church exists to fulfill the great need for love. To love and be loved is the function of God's people. God understands man's great need, and he seeks to meet that in two ways: through his Son, Jesus, and through his people, the church. What did Jesus say was the greatest commandment? " 'YOU SHALL LOVE THE LORD YOUR GOD WITH ALL YOUR HEART, AND WITH ALL YOUR SOUL, AND WITH ALL YOUR MIND.' This is the great and foremost commandment. And a second is like it, YOU SHALL LOVE YOUR NEIGHBOR AS YOURSELF" (Matt. 22: 37-39).

By loving God and being loved by him, we find the resource to love ourselves and others. Jesus said, "By this all men will know that you are My disciples, if you have love for one another" (John 13:35). The Bible says that, as believers, we are the body of Christ. This is God's way of saying that what Jesus was we are to be, and he was love.

In Chicago a young boy struggled through the snow on his way to church. He had been walking for an hour, and he was only halfway. Stopping to rest in the shelter of a doorway, a stranger asked where the boy was going. The boy said that he was on his way to Dr. Moody's church. Realizing that the young boy was passing numerous churches to get to Moody's church, the stranger asked, "Why are you so willing to walk so far?" The boy's response was a classic: "Because they really know how to love a fellow down there." The small lad had a great need for love, and the body of Christ at Moody's church knew how to meet that very basic need.

One of the finest men I have ever known is Lawrence Riley, who is eighty years old. He lives in Amory, Mississippi. Before he retired, Lawrence worked as an associate pastor of a large Baptist church in central Mississippi. While there he decided to develop a ministry with several of the nursing homes in the area. He visited weekly the folk in these various homes and shared in Bible reading and prayer. At one home was a lady who had not spoken to anyone for several years. Her children and the administrator of the nursing home said she had lost her mind. She spent her days lying in the bed, staring blankly. Brother Riley always made it a point to stop by her room for a visit. Like others before him, he would talk but would get no response. This went on for several years. One day, while sitting by her bed, Brother Riley decided he would do something different. Instead of talking to her, he started singing, "Jesus loves me! This I know, For the Bible tells me so." In the middle of his singing, the lady turned to Brother Riley, put her arms around his neck, and said, "Brother Riley, I know Jesus loves me because you do." The dear lady was not insane. She just needed to know that she was loved.

To love and to be loved is a basic need of every man. When people love, lives are changed and God is glorified.

13

Pressure, Pain, Problems

Exodus 3:11

When confronted by God's call, Moses said, "Who am I, that I should go to Pharaoh, and that I should bring the sons of Israel out of Egypt?" (Ex. 3:11). There are a number of different ways to interpret Moses' response. Could it be that Moses might have been reluctant to go back to Egypt because to do so would add pressures and problems to his life? I can just imagine Moses thinking to himself: *Lord, if I go back to Egypt, I'm just asking for migraine headaches. For me Egypt will only mean pain, pressure, and problems.*

How would you like to live without pain? You would never have a headache. Your arthritis would disappear completely. Every muscle in your body would be in perfect rhythm. Once, after a six-hour drive to Louisiana to visit my in-laws, I was stricken by a horrible headache. The pain was almost unbearable. As I attempted to get relief, I began to understand why some folk commit suicide because of intense, continuing pain. What a joy it would be never to hurt again!

How would you like to live without problems? You would have a perfect marriage in which you and your wife would live in complete harmony. Your children would obey your every wish and excel in their studies. Once a week the school teachers would call to inform you that your children were at the top of their respective classes.

Your finances would be in such good shape that it would be impossible for you to spend all your money.

How would you like to live without pressure? All your decisions would be reached by a simple deliberation. You would never be torn between conflicting ideas or emotions. You would sleep soundly for ten hours every night, and you would arise every morning with a positive attitude.

How would you like to live without pain, problems, or pressure? The way to achieve such euphoria is simple—become a corpse. I have noticed a very special characteristic of every corpse: It feels no pain, has no problems, and experiences no pressure. You can kick it, spit on it, or talk about it: it never reacts. Of course, I cannot tell you how to live *without* pain, problems, or pressure; however, I can tell you how to live *with* pain, problems, and pressure.

Perceive

You can live victoriously with pain, pressure, and problems by perceiving daily that God loves you. This is not an act based simply upon feelings. It is an act of faith based upon the Word of God. At times each of us has difficulty believing that God loves him. Guilt, failure, problems, pain, and disappointment are the devils's weapons used in a very crafty way to defeat us. The devil and his demons take much pleasure in seeing us alienated from God, from others, and from ourselves. I can assure you that the forces of evil do not want us to believe in the love of God. However, the Scriptures say, "God demonstrates His own love toward us, in that while we were yet sinners, Christ died for us" (Rom. 5:8).

Sometimes, when I am experiencing a low moment in

my life, I use my imagination in a positive way. I imagine that I am standing at the foot of the Cross. I see the body of Jesus stretched out upon that cruel tree. As I stare up into the face of Jesus, he looks at me and says, "Larry, I love you. I am dying for your sins." At other times, I imagine that it is the resurrection morning. Jesus meets me and throws his arms around my neck and whispers in my ear: "I love you." I can use my imagination in that fashion because to do so is consistent with everything I read in the Bible.

Years ago, a pastor was in a hospital recuperating from a serious illness. As his body healed, he attempted to meet other patients and to give them a word of encouragement. One morning he met a lady who was in a wheelchair and who was in much pain. She asked him, "If there is a God of love, why does he allow people to suffer?"

Since the lady was very bitter, the pastor was careful in his response. He asked the lady, "Do you believe that suffering is a fact?"

For thirty minutes the woman described her three months in the hospital. She related in vivid detail all the hurt and suffering she had seen. Finally, in a state of exhaustion, she ceased speaking.

Very gently the pastor remarked, "We both agree that suffering is a fact. Now try to explain this suffering without God. Can suffering be explained by denying God's love? Is suffering more acceptable when we deny his existence?"

Rejecting God because pain, problems, and pressures exist does not make life easier. On the contrary, such a disposition compounds our problems. If, in the midst of our sufferings, we believe in a God who deeply loves us, we find the strength to deal with our adversities. Like the apostle Paul we can say, "But in all these things we over-whelmingly conquer through Him who loved us" (Rom. 8:37).

Pray

We can live victoriously with pain, problems, and pressures if we pray daily from a thankful heart. This is a command of the Scriptures. The apostle Paul said,

"Rejoice in the Lord always; again I will say, rejoice! Let your forbearing *spirit* be known to all men. The Lord is near. Be anxious for nothing, but in everything by prayer and supplication with thanksgiving let your requests be made known to God. And the peace of God, which surpasses all comprehension, shall guard your hearts and your minds in Christ Jesus" (Phil. 4:4-7).

The apostle Paul had more than his share of pain, problems, and pressure. In almost every major city where Paul preached, he met fierce opposition. He was jailed, stoned, beaten, and cursed. Some of his associates forsook him. Others were jealous of his leadership and attempted to undermine his ministry. Apparently Paul practiced what he preached in the Philippian letter. His victorious life, in the face of pain, pressure, and problems, is clearly seen in his writing. "*We are* afflicted in every way, but not crushed; perplexed, but not despairing; persecuted, but not forsaken; struck down, but not destroyed; always carrying about in the body the dying of Jesus, that the life of Jesus also may be manifested in our body" (2 Cor. 4:8-10).

If we are to pray daily from a thankful heart, we must major on the positive and not the negative. A husband informed his wife he was leaving her for another woman. A marriage of ten years was dissolved overnight. The hurt and shame was so great that during the following months the wife was in despair. One afternoon, while sitting near the beach with her children, she read a book in which the author suggested that in difficult moments a person should make a list of all the good things in his life. The idea at first appeared ridiculous, but she thought, *What do I have to lose?* For three hours she listed all the pluses in her life. In relating that experience she wrote: "Granted, it was a very small beginning. But it did light a tiny flame in me. The next year and a half was horrible . . . . But I knew from that moment on the beach that through divine power I was going to make it. And I did . . . when my friends turn to me with sorrows and dismay I always repeat the story of my list that day on the beach."[1]

If you expect the best, you will probably get it. On the other hand, if you expect the worst, you will probably get that. I am reminded of a young woman who had a special problem. Upon returning from her honeymoon, she and her husband settled down for the first night in their new home. Within minutes after the bedroom lights were turned out, the new bride informed her husband that she was sure she heard a thief prowling in the living room. The young husband got out of bed and went downstairs, but he could not find any evidence of a prowler. This went on for seventeen years. Always the patient husband returned to the bedroom to inform his wife that no prowler was in the house. One night while the husband was checking the rooms at the request of his wife, he discovered a thief. Catching the prowler by surprise, the husband said, "Sir, don't be alarmed. Take anything you want. But when you get through, will you please come up to my bedroom and meet my wife. She has been looking for you for seventeen years!"

Perform

You can live victoriously with pain, problems, and pressures if you make it a habit to perform acts of love for others. Within our church family we have many people who are carrying heavy burdens. Those who carry their burdens best are those who are helping to carry the burdens of others. The folk who are busy helping with the hurts of their neighbors really do not have time to sit around and feel sorry for themselves. These folk invest their personalities in behalf of others who are also fighting pains and problems.

Many years ago Bill Stidger, a famous preacher, went into a deep depression. The concern and interest of friends had little effect on his condition. A fellow pastor visited Stidger and suggested that he write thank-you notes to those who had blessed his life in past years. Stidger gave the idea some thought and decided to write his high school English teacher. She helped him develop a love for literature that he had never lost. He wasn't even sure she was still alive, for he had not seen her in many years. He wrote to her, expressing his appreciation for her ministry in his life.

A few days later Stidger received a letter from his former teacher:

Dear Willie:

Thank you for the note of kindness. It meant so much. You are the first student in 50 years to write me a letter of appreciation. You will never know how much I shall treasure this letter.

Stidger said that somewhere between that letter and the other 499 he wrote, he came out of his depression. When we invest our lives in others, we find the strength to deal with our problems and pressures.

Can it be true that sometimes God allows problems to come into our lives so that we can become better ministers to those who have similar problems? The apostle Paul said,

"Blessed *be* the God and Father of our Lord Jesus Christ, the Father of mercies and God of all comfort; who comforts us in all our affliction so that we may be able to comfort those who are in any affliction with the comfort with which we ourselves are comforted by God" (2 Cor. 1:3-4).

There is no way to live without pain, problems, or pressures; however, when we are convinced of God's love, pray daily from a thankful heart, and perform acts of love for others, we will find the strength to live victoriously in spite of our hurts and disappointments. We are more than conquerors through Christ who loves us.

14

The Enriched Marriage

Exodus 4:24-26

In relating Moses' return to Egypt, the Bible records a strange experience:

"Now it came about at the lodging place on the way that the LORD met him and sought to put him to death. Then Zipporah took a flint and cut off her son's foreskin and threw *it* at Moses' feet, and she said, 'You are indeed a bridegroom of blood to me.' So He let him alone" (Ex. 4:24-26).

The biblical record seems to show that Moses had problems in his marriage. Quite possibly he had an unhappy marriage. Exactly what caused the unhappiness is not clear. The above Scripture passage indicates that part of the problem was of a religious nature. Seemingly, Zipporah had opposed the Hebrew rite of circumcision, and this had created a barrier between God and Moses. After this incident, Zipporah passed from the scene.

This experience in the life of Moses should remind all of us that the best of people may have problems in marriage. Moses was a great man of God; but he, too, had his marriage problems. As I grow older I am much more sympathetic toward those who have felt the necessity for divorce. Divorce does not necessarily mean that there is a moral problem. After marriage, some folk discover that their backgrounds and attitudes toward life are incompatible.

Although I do not encourage divorce, and I do my best to help people build a lasting marriage, there are times when I realize that continuation will only lead to more problems.

As we reflect upon the experience of Moses, we are compelled to ask: What helps to make a marriage successful? A person might respond love is necessary. Recently the question was asked: What is the difference between infatuation and love? One wise individual responded: "Infatuation is when you think he is as sexy as Robert Redford, as smart as Henry Kissinger, as noble as Ralph Nader, as funny as Woody Allen, and as athletic as Jimmy Conners. However, it is love when you realize that he is as sexy as Woody Allen, as smart as Jimmy Conners, as funny as Ralph Nader, as athletic as Henry Kissinger, and he doesn't look anything like Robert Redford—but, you will take him anyway."[1] Another wise person once said that love is "when it's 10 PM, and you get this gnawing need for peach ice cream, and even though you're not sick or pregnant, he drives to a drugstore and buys you some."[2]

One day a Catholic priest asked a little girl for the definition of matrimony. She said, "Oh, matrimony is a state of terrible torment where you have to go before you enter heaven."

The priest responded, "No dear, you gave me the definition for purgatory—I asked for matrimony."

The archbishop who had been listening said, "Be quiet, she knows more than we do."

How are we to build a growing and successful marriage?

Courtship

Courtship is important in the growth of a successful marriage. If husbands and wives are to grow in their marriage relationships, they must realize the importance of keeping romance alive. In my first pastorate after graduation from the seminary, I was privileged to know Garth and Margie Crumby. I quickly discovered that these were folk who worked at keeping romance alive in their marriage. They had four beautiful children, all of whom are married now and doing quite well. Margie and Garth always took two vacations. First, they took the whole family to the coast and had a wonderful time together. Then they reserved a second week just for themselves. They knew how to enjoy each other's company. Garth was always praising Margie, and she, in turn, praised him. On numerous occasions I saw Garth put his arm around Margie and praise her before others. Courtship was a building block in their growing marriage.

Sometimes our family backgrounds make it difficult for us to practice courtship. Muriel James demonstrates this truth in the story of Howard. Howard was the only child. He was born to his parents when they were in their forties. Howard remembered that his parents were aloof and displayed very little affection for him or between themselves. His father always said, "Public display of affection is in poor taste." He remembered his father, saying to his mother, "Alice, don't kiss me in front of the child. No telling what he might think." Howard found it very difficult to practice courtship because his "parent-tape" in his mind would not allow him. With help Howard was able to turn off the old "parent-tape" and express his feelings openly.[3]

In practicing courtship folk must learn to look their best. If you are a parent of small children, you will have to work extra hard. Don't say it can't be done. Remember it is your marriage. You can make it or break it. Couples need to go out and do things together. Although most of us do not have the resources to go to Hawaii, we can go out for an evening meal. Simple things done repeatedly build a healthy marriage.

Praise is an important part of courtship. Look for the good qualities in your spouse and praise him for it. Marabel Morgan has observed:

Tomorrow morning watch your husband when he looks in the mirror. He sees an eighteen-year-old youth with firm stomach muscles and a full head of hair. No matter what his age, he doesn't see his pouch or his receding hairline. He sees what he wants to see, and wants you to see that eighteen-year old, too. Of course, this isn't really so strange. What age girl do you see in the mirror? My own grandmother admitted to me feeling that she was not much past 21.[4]

A dear wife, who wanted to improve the courtship in her marriage, decided she would seek ways in which to praise her husband. Although he had slim arms, she squeezed his muscle and thanked him for being such a strong person. The next night, when she called him to the dinner table, he was nowhere to be found. Going out into the garage, she found him lifting weights. He wanted to build up more muscles for her to admire.[5]

When it comes to praise, women are no different from men. Take the time to notice the dress your wife is wearing and brag on her appearance. Take special care to praise her work in the home. Every word of kindness is a building block in a growing marriage. As one wife said,

"When he says he loves you, he should always give a lot of details: why does he love you? How much does he love you? When and where did he first begin to love you? Favorable comparisons with all other women he ever loved also are welcome, even though he insists it would take forever to count the ways in which he loves you, you wouldn't want to discourage him from counting."[6]

Dan Morton, pastor of First Baptist Church, Indianola, Mississippi, tells the story of a couple who divorced. He took one son; she took the other. He lived at one end of the street; she lived at the other end. At no time did they communicate. In his old age the husband became a Christian and made a definite change in his life-style. He became very close to his sons; however, his wife refused to have anything to do with him. Upon his death, the sons arranged a proper funeral. At the insistence of the sons, the mother came to the funeral home but refused to view the body. The casket was opened for the last time. The sons stood over the body, weeping profusely. At the last moment the mother, who had remained at the rear of the funeral home, got up and walked toward the casket. Stopping about six feet from the casket, she raised her hands and said, "Farewell and good riddance." She was a lady who wasn't capable of communicating.

Communication does not come easy. One must work at it. First, it involves time. Couples must decide to set aside a few moments for themselves. If there are children in the family, the time will probably come late at night or after the children have gone to school in the morning. This special time can be a moment when the day's events are discussed.

Second, communication involves speaking and listening. It is a time of sharing, and it is a time of listening. Too often the counselor hears the complaint, "He never listens to a word I say." I have a feeling that women sometimes fall in love with their doctors and preachers because these men listen to what the women have to say.

Third, communication involves openness. It is the willingness to listen and appreciate what the other person is saying. A lady said to her pastor, "Ed and I never argue. Occasionally, we have a little difference of opinion; but we never disagree because Ed sees that I am right and he shuts up.''

The pastor responded, "What happens when Ed is right?" "Oh," she said, "Ed is never right.''

Silence and arrogance are great killers of marriage. Tragically, too many couples excel in silence. The biblical record would indicate that Moses and Zipporah probably failed to communicate.

Confession

Confession is important in the growth of a successful marriage. By *confession* I mean a willingness to say, I am sorry. Marriages that are growing in maturity are marked by confession and forgiveness. Love grows where people are willing to confess and to forgive.

I read that 80 percent of all second marriages are successful. I have a feeling that is because people have learned from the previous marriage the importance of confession and forgiveness.

A young husband decided to put new carpet in his home, and he was determined to do it alone. He worked very hard. At the completion of his project, he admired his work with a great sense of accomplishment. Before he called his wife in to see his masterpiece, he noticed a small lump in the carpet. He wasn't about to remove the carpet, and he certainly did not want his wife to see his error. Walking over to the small lump, he got down on his hands and knees and started pressing out the lump with his hands and feet. He then called his wife to come and admire his work. As she gazed at the beautiful carpet, he asked, "Honey, have you seen my cigarettes?"

She replied, "Yes, I see them over there on the windowsill." Then she asked, "By the way, Darling, have you seen the parakeet?"

Every marriage will have its share of parakeets under the carpet. All of us make mistakes, and all of us must learn to confess and to forgive.

Years ago a movie became famous for the saying, "Love is never having to say you are sorry." In response to that remark, an astute wife contended: "Love means never having to say you're sorry except when it's your fault. Or when it's his fault but he's too immature to admit it. Or when it's the children's fault but he's holding you responsible. Or when it's nobody's fault but he's looking for a scapegoat. Or when . . . ."[7]

Couples who practice confession and forgiveness are establishing a foundation that will help in the building of a growing marriage. As the apostle Paul said, "Be kind to one another, tender-hearted, forgiving each other, just as God in Christ also has forgiven you" (Eph. 4:32).

On their fiftieth wedding anniversary, a couple summed up the reasons for their successful marriage. The husband remarked, "I have tried never to be selfish. After all, there is no *I* in the word 'marriage.' "

The wife responded, "For my part, I have never corrected my husband's spelling."

Communion

Communion with God is important in the growth of a successful marriage. A marriage counselor once asked 750 couples to state what they thought was the greatest factor for happiness in their family lives. The counselor reported that the vast majority said, "Religion lived daily in the home."[8]

Communion with God means, first of all, that we make a sincere commitment to Jesus Christ. The Philippian jailer asked, "Sirs, what must I do to be saved? And they said, 'Believe in the Lord Jesus' " (Acts 16:30-31). A

Christian marriage is composed of two people who are believing in a living Jesus and allow that Jesus into their lives. They are in communion and intimate fellowship with the living Lord.

Second, communion with God involves worship. A Christian marriage is composed of two people who take the time to worship together, to pray together, and to study God's Word together. Joyce Landorff described *communion* when she said,

"We need to experience a time of worship to God in his house, to tithe a tenth or more of our income, to give him gifts above our tithe, and to hear the singing of the choir and congregation. We need to be warmed by a friend leaning over our pew who whispers, 'All week I've been thinking about you and have been holding you up in prayer before our Lord.' We need the message that streams forth out of the heart of our pastor, and we need the presence of each other if we are to survive another week."[9]

Several years ago Louis Evans wrote a book entitled, *Your Marriage, Duel or Duet?* It is a good book; however, marriage was never intended to be a duet. It was intended to be a trio. A triangle can also represent marriage. The sides are represented by the husband and wife; the base of the triangle is Christ. When marriage becomes a triangle, there is always hope for a growing marriage because the union is on God's foundation.

It is not easy to build a growing marriage, and we need to be more sympathetic with those who have failed in their marriages. Let us offer our hands to those who are struggling. With God's help through courtship, communication, confession, and communion, let us use these building blocks for a marriage of our own that is growing and maturing.

15

Lessons from a Shepherd's Staff

Exodus 4:1-4

As God prepared Moses for the task of leading the Hebrews out of Egypt, he gave him a sign of authority. The Bible states:

Then Moses answered and said, "What if they will not believe me, or listen to what I say? For they may say, 'The LORD has not appeared to you.' " And the LORD said to him, "What is that in your hand?" And he said, "A staff." Then He said, "Throw it on the ground." So he threw it on the ground, and it became a serpent; and Moses fled from it. But the LORD said to Moses, "Stretch out your hand and grasp *it* by its tail"—so he stretched out his hand and caught it, and it became a staff in his hand (Ex. 4:1-4).

Many famous generals and soldiers have been known for their unique dress and style. General George Patton is remembered for his fiery temper and the pearl-handled Colt .45s. General Douglas MacArthur will always be remembered for his flamboyancy and his frayed general's cap and old pipe. Teddy Roosevelt is remembered for the phrase: "Speak softly but carry a big stick."

Although Moses did not have a Colt .45 or a pipe, he certainly carried a big stick—a shepherd's staff. There are several lessons we can learn from Moses and his shepherd's staff.

God Can Use What We Have

The first lesson we can learn from the shepherd's staff is that God can use what we have for good. When Moses met God in the desert, Moses possessed very little in material goods. About the only think he had were the clothes on his back and a common shepherd's staff. However, the staff was really all God needed. In the days that followed, Moses saw God energize his staff to defy a king and divide a sea. This reminds us that if we are willing to submit to God's leadership, God can use the most common things in our lives as a means of expressing his divine power.

In John 6 the beloved apostle tells us that on one occasion, with a few loaves and two fishes, Jesus fed over five thousand people. As the dinner hour approached, Jesus suggested to the disciples that the time had come to feed the hungry crowd. The disciples could not see how that could be accomplished. Fearing that the incident might make Jesus look bad, they suggested that the crowd be sent away (Matt. 14:15). When it was obvious that Jesus was not going to leave, a small boy offered his lunch which consisted of five barley loaves and two fish. Although the boy did not have much, it was all that Jesus needed to feed the multitude. A miracle took place that day, and when all had been fed, "They gathered them up, and filled twelve baskets with fragments from the five barley loaves, which were left over by those who had eaten" (John 6:13). Yes, God is able to take what we have and use it for much good.

A very dear lady in our church recently said to me that she felt useless because she had very little to offer the world. Since this lady was involved in our outreach ministry, I knew she was making a contribution in life. A few days later I was visiting an elderly lady at the nursing home. During the course of our conversation, she referred to the lady who felt she was not doing anything worthwhile. This beloved saint said of her: "You know she has the most wonderful smile. Everytime she smiles at me I feel good all over." God can take a simple thing like a smile and light up a lonely life. The shepherd's staff, five loaves of bread and two fish, and a smile remind us that God can use the simple things of life to work great miracles.

All of Us Want to Hide Sometimes

The Bible says that when Moses threw down his staff, "It became a serpent; and Moses fled from it" (Ex. 4:3). I really don't blame Moses; I would have done the same. I wonder how far he ran before he stopped?

Have you ever wanted to run away and hide? Has life ever been so unbearable that you simply wanted to become anonymous? The second truth we can learn from the shepherd's staff is that there are times when all of us want to run and hide. The greatest of God's prophets have had this desire. Elijah was a courageous prophet. On one occasion he challenged the prophets of Baal and secured a mighty victory. But then Queen Jezebel, who was promoting Baal worship, let it be known that she was going to kill the prophet. When Elijah heard the queen's edict, the Bible says,

He was afraid and arose and ran for his life and came to Beersheba, which belongs to Judah, and left his servant there. But he himself went a day's journey into the wilderness, and came and sat down under a juniper tree; and he requested for himself that he might die (1 Kings 19:3-4).

At some point in life, most of us have to face a Jezebel. Don't be surprised if you feel like running away and hiding when you are confronted by a Jezebel.

Jonah was commissioned by God to preach to the wicked city of Nineveh. In response to God's call, "Jonah rose up to flee to Tarshish from the presence of the LORD" (Jonah 1:3). The prophet had no desire to preach to the hated Ninevehites, and he felt his only alternative was anonymity in Tarshish. Have you ever run from God's will?

When Jesus was arrested, Peter sought to defend Jesus. Peter unleashed his sword and cut off the ear of a servant of the high priest; he probably aimed for the head and missed. To Peter's astonishment, Jesus did not resist his captors, and he instructed Peter to put away his sword. The disciples were confused and afraid and could not understand the submissive attitude of Jesus. The Bible says, "all the disciples left Him and fled" (Matt. 26:56). And a few hours later, as the trial of Jesus reached its climax, a young woman asked Peter if he were a follower of Jesus. Hiding behind a curtain of curses, he shouted, "I do not know the man" (Matt. 26:74).

Guilt, fear, failure, anger, tragedy, and disappointments can cause the best of us to run and hide. Dr. James Dobson reminds us that young people want to run away and hide because of deep feelings of inferiority:

You are 16 years old and your name is Helen Highschool. To be honest, you are not exactly gorgeous. Your shoulders are rounded and you have trouble remembering to close your mouth when you're thinking. (That seems to worry your folks a lot.) There are pimples distributed at random over your forehead and chin, and your oversized ears keep peeking out from under the hair that should hide them. You think often about these flaws and have wondered, with proper reverence, why God wasn't paying more attention when you were being assembled.

You've never had a real date in your life, except for that

disaster last February. Your Mom's friend, Mrs. Nowsgood, arranged a blind date that almost signaled the end of the world. You knew it was risky to accept, but you were too excited to think rationally. Charming Charley arrived in high spirits expecting to meet the girl of his dreams. You were not what he had in mind. Do you remember the disappointment on his face when you shuffled into the living room? . . . . The night of your date he didn't say anything! He just sulked through the evening and brought you home two hours early![1]

I read about a mother who was so overwhelmed by the responsibility of rearing four small children that she crawled under the covers and refused to get out of bed. All of us have times when life becomes so unbearable that we feel compelled to drop out of the human race. Even if you feel this way, don't give up. There is hope for you.

We Can Do the Impossible

Moses ran, but God called him back. The Lord said to Moses: " 'Stretch out your hand and grasp *it* by its tail'— so he stretched out his hand and caught it, and it became a staff in his hand" (Ex. 4:4). Have you ever attempted to catch a poisonous snake by its tail? The impossibility of that task was impressed upon me this past summer when I visited Silver Springs, Florida. While there I saw a young man exhibit eight live rattlesnakes. Clothed in heavy boots and using a long pole, the young man explained to the audience the various characteristics of a rattlesnake. On several occasions he angered the snakes causing them to strike. The snakes struck so quickly that only the breaking of a balloon permitted the audience to realize that the snakes had struck. As I watched the deadly rattlesnakes, I thought of Moses.

From a human standpoint which was more impossible,

to free the Hebrews from the greatest military power in the world or to grab a snake by its tail? With God's help both were possible. When Moses picked up the snake by its tail, God was saying that Moses had the authority to lead God's people out of bondage.

While watching Robert Schuller's TV program *The Hour of Power*, I heard a testimony about God's power to help a man do the impossible. A pastor with mechanical arms and hands was standing with Schuller. Several years ago this pastor had resigned a large church in order to work with retarded children. He dreamed of building a ranch in Arizona to serve as a home where these children could grow and develop. Selling everything he owned, he bought land in Arizona and attempted to erect his first building. While working one day, he received an electric shock which caused him to lose both hands and arms. You can imagine his discouragement and despair; however, he refused to give up. With mechanical arms and hands he continued his work. Various state newspapers featured articles on his life, and soon thousands of donations were made to his project. He had originally hoped to have his home on a sound operating basis within ten to fifteen years. However, hundreds of thousands of dollars were given and within a short period of time the retarded children's home was in full operation. Like Moses, that handicapped pastor had been able to grab the snake in his life by its tail; God used mechanical arms and hands to turn the desert into a beautiful ranch of love. That pastor had a handicapped body, but he did not have a handicapped faith. With God's help he did the impossible.

Elijah was eventually able to face Jezebel. Jonah was able to preach in Nineveh, and Peter was able to witness for Christ. God gave them the strength to do what they thought was impossible, and he will do the same for you.

The Source of Our Strength Is God

The fourth lesson we can learn from this experience in the life of Moses is that the source of our strength is God. Every time Moses leaned on that shepherd's staff, he was reminded that God was his strength. Jonah, Elijah, and Peter experienced those moments when they felt compelled to run and hide; however, like Moses, they were able to return and succeed because God was their strength.

Luther Bridgers was a great evangelistic singer. While away in a revival meeting one week, he received word that his wife and two children had burned to death in a fire. Crushed by the news, he ran out into the night in a state of shock. Coming to a river, he gave serious consideration to taking his own life. In a matter of minutes he could be reunited with his family. But God would not let him go. Dropping to his knees, he poured out his heart to God. He asked for God's strength to deal with tragedy. The struggle was long and difficult, but slowly he was able to find his way back.

Eventually, he remarried and reared a second family. As he contemplated how God had seen him through a tragic experience, he wrote a hymn that has become known to all Christians around the world:

> Jesus, Jesus, Jesus,
> Sweetest name I know,
> Fills my ev'ry longing,
> Keeps me singing as I go.[2]

From Moses' shepherd's staff we learn that God can use what we have. There are times when we want to hide, but with God's help we can do the impossible. The source of our strength is God. The Lord can keep us singing as we go forward in his will.

16

Between a Rock
and a Hard Place

Exodus 5:21-23

In 480 BC, the Persians under King Xerxes attempted to capture the city states of Greece. Xerxes' father, Darius, had attempted the same thing in 490 BC but had failed. As the huge Persian army advanced through northern Greece, Leonidas, a Greek soldier, took three hundred Spartan warriors and advanced to the narrow coastal plain at Thermopylae. Thermopylae was nothing more than a fifty-foot-wide beach between the mountain and the sea. It was an excellent defensive position where a small force could hold off a much larger army. In preparation for the battle, the Spartan soldiers combed their hair. Upon hearing of this Xerxes laughed, but he was later informed that he should take the event more seriously because it meant the Spartans were preparing to die.

Prior to the battle, a Greek traitor revealed to the Persians a secret trail around the mountain which enabled the Persians to strike from the front and rear. When the sun arose on the day of the battle, King Leonidas discovered that he and his three hundred men were surrounded. They were caught between a rock and a hard place.

Upon Moses' return to Egypt, the Hebrews received him with open arms. They were impressed with his unusual shepherd's staff and were convinced that the Egyptians would be overthrown immediately. However, Pharaoh, who was not impressed with Moses, decided to increase

the burdens of the Hebrew slaves. It was not long before
the Hebrews were blaming Moses for all their problems.
They suggested that he might do everyone a favor by dis-
appearing into the wilderness for a second time. The Bible
says

"Moses returned to the LORD and said, 'O LORD, why
hast Thou brought harm to this people? Why didst Thou
ever send me? Ever since I came to Pharaoh to speak in
Thy name, he has done harm to this people; and Thou hast
not delivered Thy people at all' " (Ex. 5:22-23).

Moses was caught between a rock and a hard place.
Have you ever had a similar experience? What do you do
when you are caught between a rock and a hard place?

Talk to God

I never shall forget the first time our older son learned
to climb out of his baby bed. After hitting the floor, he
came running into our bedroom and said with a big smile,
"Good morning, ladies and gentlemen." I have a feeling
that Moses desperately wanted to see a smiling face that
would say, good morning. But no such human face
existed. Caught between a rock and a hard place Moses
did the right thing: He talked to God.

When caught in a squeeze, the world seems to say,
When in trouble, when in doubt, run in circles, scream and
shout. The Bible says that when you find yourself in a
squeeze, take the time to talk to God.

Philippians 4 tells us that when we are caught in a
squeeze not to go to pieces but to turn to God in prayer:
"Be anxious for nothing, but in everything by prayer and
supplication with thanksgiving let your requests be made
known to God. And the peace of God . . . shall guard
your hearts and your minds in Christ Jesus" (Phil. 4:6-7).

In Acts 16 we are informed that Paul and Silas were thrown in prison for preaching the gospel. While in prison they put into practice their preaching and refused to be anxious. "Paul and Silas were praying and singing hymns of praise to God, and the prisoners were listening to them" (Acts 16:25).

In writing to Timothy, the apostle Paul said that he had been abandoned and that ruthless men were working against him. However, the apostle must have talked to God because he said, "At my first defense no one supported me, but all deserted me; . . . . But the Lord stood with me, and strengthened me, in order that through me the proclamation might be fully accomplished" (2 Tim. 4:16-17). The words "stood" and "strengthened" remind us that God can help us when we are caught between a rock and a hard place.

In May of 1940, the battered British Army was stranded on the beaches of Dunkirk. Hitler's war machine was before them, and in the rear was the English Channel. Caught between a rock and a hard place, the army and all of England prayed for God's help. In every boat and ship that would float, English citizens floated across the channel to rescue the helpless army. Most of the army was rescued by a miracle of God, and England survived to fight another day.

Yes, when you find yourself caught in a squeeze, take the time to talk to God.

Listen to God

When you are caught between a rock and a hard place, it is always wise to listen to God. The Scriptures declare that as Moses pled his case before God, he heard God say, "I am the LORD" (Ex. 6:2). We must realize that God is the Lord of the universe. He is in control. God doesn't have any problems, just solutions. Moses was reminded that God had already prepared a plan that would bring victory to God's people.

When we find ourselves caught in a squeeze, we do ourselves a great favor if we take the time to listen to God. Like the psalmist we can learn to say:

> God is our refuge and strength,
> A very present help in trouble.
> Therefore we will not fear, though the earth should
>   change,
> And though the mountains slip into the heart of the
>   sea;
> Though its waters roar *and* foam,
> Though the mountains quake at its swelling pride
>   (Ps. 46:1-3).

In our moments of doubt and fear we need to hear Jesus say: "I will not leave you as orphans; I will come to you. After a little while the world will behold Me no more; but you *will* behold Me; because I live, you shall live also" (John 14:18-19). In Jesus' time there were no homes or institutions for fatherless children. Orphans were almost defenseless against a cruel and sinful world. Captured for slaves and abused as animals, orphans were helpless figures in the Roman age. In his last hour, Jesus assured his followers that he would not abandon them. His Spirit would come to give strength for living. This same Jesus lives today, reminding us that he has not left us to exist as helpless orphans.

The apostle Paul suffered greatly from a disease that is never named. Life appeared to be squeezing in on him. In desperation he prayed, seeking God's help. He tells us that God did not promise healing, but he did hear God say, "My grace is sufficient for you" (2 Cor. 12:9). When caught between a rock and hard place, we can discover that God's grace is sufficient for the hour.

Alexander Solzhenitsyn has related many of the difficult ordeals faced by men in the prison camps of the Soviet Union. In stressing the power of spiritual values, he tells of a fellow prisoner who seemed to live victoriously in the midst of all the misery of the prison camp. Every night after this man crawled into his cot, he read from a crumpled piece of paper. While the man was reading, his face would shine with joy. Solzhenitsyn later discovered that the verses from the Bible were written on the paper. When caught between a rock and a hard place, this man had learned to listen to God.

Trust Yourself to God

When caught between a rock and a hard place, put your trust in God. Moses did. Trusting God's leadership, Moses returned to God's people and to Pharaoh. In our moments of doubt and depression, we need to remind ourselves that we are "superconquerors" through Jesus Christ. Paul listed a series of things that can make any Christian feel as if he is caught between a rock and a hard place. He asked, "Who shall separate us from the love of Christ? Shall tribulation, or distress, or persecution, or famine, or nakedness, or peril, or sword? But in all these things we overwhelmingly conquer through Him who loved us" (Rom. 8:35,37). The expression, "we overwhelmingly conquer," is only one word in the Greek— *hupernikomen*. It means to conquer completely. If you were comparing the meaning of this word, *hupernikomen*, to a football score, it would be expressed as 100 to 0.

In the year 490 BC, the Persians attempted to conquer the Greeks. Under the leadership of Miltiades, the Greeks met the Persian army on the plain of Marathon. Instead of establishing defensive positions, the Greek army attacked; the Persians were caught off guard. The attack was so ferocious that the Persians were almost annihilated. The Greek historian, Herodotus wrote that the Greek army lost 192 men; the Persians lost 6,400 men. On that day the Greeks were superconquerors. Just as the Greeks were able to conquer the Persians at Marathon, so Christ empowers us to be victorious in life. As we trust ourselves to him, he is able to win the victory. This was true for Moses, and it can be true for us.

When we find ourselves between a rock and a hard place, let us talk to God, listen to God, and trust ourselves to God. The Lord will give us the strength we need.

17

When God Does Not Divide the Waters

Exodus 14:21-22

After bringing destruction upon the Egyptians through a series of devastating plagues, Moses led the Hebrews out of Egypt to the Red Sea. As the Egyptian army approached from the rear, the Bible says,

"Moses stretched out his hand over the sea; and the LORD swept the sea *back* by a strong east wind all night, and turned the sea into dry land, so the waters were divided. And the sons of Israel went through the midst of the sea on the dry land, and the waters *were like* a wall to them on their right hand and on their left" (Ex. 14:21-22).

Upon returning from Sunday School, a little boy was asked by his parents to explain what he had learned in Sunday School. The lad said that the Sunday School lesson had been about Moses crossing the Red Sea. He said, "Moses called the astronauts in Houston, Texas, for assistance. They flew over to Egypt in a jumbo jet and erected a steel bridge. Moses was able then to move his army and tanks to the other side."

The mother responded, "Now, Son, you know that your Sunday School teacher did not tell you that story."

"I know," he said, "but if I were to tell you what she told me, you would never believe it."

Do you believe God divided the waters? One day a professor was explaining to his class that Moses did not literally divide the waters of the Red Sea. He contended that the water was very shallow and that Moses and his people walked through water about ankle deep. As the professor gave his logical explanation, a student in the back of the classroom shouted, "Amen and praise the Lord."

The teacher was surprised at that response. He walked to the rear of the room and asked, "Why are you praising God?"

The young man replied, "Well, if what you said is true, that is a greater miracle than the parting of the Red Sea."

The teacher responded, "How can that be?"

"If what you said is true, that means the Egyptian army drowned in six inches of water," the student answered.

From this experience in the life of Moses, three important truths become apparent.

Sometimes God Does Divide the Waters

If the Bible is true, and I believe it is, there was a day under the leadership of Moses when God divided the waters of the Red Sea, enabling God's people to walk on dry land to the other side. It was a miracle of God, and it impresses upon all of us that God is able to work miracles for his people.

In Daniel 6 we are informed that Daniel was thrown in a lions' den because of his religious convictions. The Scripture states: "Then the king gave orders, and Daniel was brought in and cast into the lions' den" (Dan. 6:16). However, the next morning, when the king arrived at the lions' den, he heard Daniel say, "My God sent His angel and shut the lions' mouths, and they have not harmed me" (Dan. 6:22).

Shirley P. Wheeler believed that God could shut the mouths of lions. Back in the mid 1890s, she and her six-year-old sister were walking on a country road in Pennsylvania. Shirley was nine, and she and her sister were having a carefree time among chattering squirrels and singing birds. The girls had been picking wild berries, when all at once they came upon a huge panther. He was lying on a flat rock, and his large yellow eyes were glued on the girls. Instinctively, Shirley said to her sister, "Don't look at him." She whispered to her sister to keep walking and prayed within her heart for God's protection. Someone had told her that wild animals would not attack a human being who was singing. Holding her sister by the hand and walking straight ahead, Shirley started singing:

> There is sunshine in my soul today.
> When Jesus shows His smiling face,
> There is sunshine in my soul.

Shirley said that, as they walked past the beast, she could feel its hot breath upon her neck. The panther gazed at them with intense curiosity but made no move to attack. Finally, after what seemed like hours but actually was only seconds, they walked out of view of the panther. Later that day the panther was killed. It measured eight feet and three inches in length.

Shirley Wheeler eventually became a doctor. She lived to be ninety years old. Shirley never had any trouble believing that God closed the mouths of the lions for Daniel.[1]

In Acts 12 we are informed that God delivered Peter from jail. The church was praying for him:

Behold, an angel of the LORD suddenly appeared, and a light shone in the cell; and he struck Peter's side and roused him, saying, "Get up quickly." And his chains fell off his hands . . . . They came to the iron gate that leads into the city, which opened for them by itself; and they went out and went along one street; and immediately the angel departed from him (Acts 12:7, 10).

The account given in Acts 12 reminds me of a missionary's testimony which I heard at the Southern Baptist Convention several years ago. A missionary, who had served in Viet Nam, told how on one occasion the Vietcong broke into his home. They bound him and attempted to rape his wife. Not knowing what to do and feeling totally helpless, he shouted, "In the name of Jesus leave my wife alone." The Vietcong became silent and appeared to be very confused. After a few moments, they walked slowly out of the house and disappeared into the jungle. This missionary was convinced that God could divide the waters.

God Does Not Always Divide the Waters

As we ponder the miracle that God worked for Moses and the Hebrews at the Red Sea, we are reminded that God does not always divide the waters as we would wish. Acts 12 tells us of Peter's deliverance from jail and of James' death: "Now about that time Herod the king laid hands on some who belonged to the church, in order to mistreat them. And he had James the brother of John put to death with a sword" (Acts 12:1-2). I feel certain that the church prayed for James; however, he was not delivered and he died for his faith.

In the garden of Gethsemane Jesus asked, "My father, if it is possible, let this cup pass from Me" (Matt. 26:39). However, Jesus came to realize that it was not God's will to remove the Cross. For him, the waters were not divided.

In Acts 7 we are introduced to Stephen, one of the great deacons of the early church. He was a man filled with compassion and courage. He loved Jesus and had a burning heart that compelled him to share Christ with others. He was a pillar of strength, who must have been a tremendous inspiration to the other believers. Speaking before the Sanhedrin, he proclaimed Jesus as the Son of God; however, when he gave the invitation the Bible says "they cried out with a loud voice, and covered their ears, and they rushed upon him with one impulse. And they went on stoning Stephen as he called upon *the Lord* and said, 'Lord Jesus, receive my spirit!' " (Acts 7:57,59). For him, the waters were not divided.

Most of us have heard the thrilling story of how Jim Elliott and other missionaries penetrated the Amazon jungle to share Christ with the Auca Indians. For years they had prayed and planned for the moment when they could share Christ with this Stone Age tribe. Waiting on a sandy beach near a jungle river, they radioed home that the Aucas appeared friendly; however, under the guise of friendship the Aucas attacked and killed Jim Elliott and the other missionaries. For these men, God did not divide the waters.

Strength to Stand on the Shore

If God does not divide the waters as we would wish, he will give us the strength to stand on the shore. The heavenly Father gave Jesus and Stephen the strength to die as believers. From the Cross Jesus was heard to say, "Father, forgive them; for they do not know what they are doing" (Luke 23:34). You can imagine the surprise of the Sanhedrin when they heard Stephen cry, "Lord, do not hold this sin against them!" (Acts 7:60). Although God did not divide the waters of life for them, he did divide death and bring them into his eternal kingdom.

Jim Elliott and his missionary friends died in the jungle.

Later, however, Elizabeth Elliott made contact with the Auca tribe. God empowered her to stand on the shore. She was able to lead to Christ the Indian who had personally killed her husband.

For many years Jeff Ray was professor of preaching at Southwestern Baptist Theological Seminary. His wife died when his children were very young. His son was murdered years later, and the crime was never solved. The tragic death of his son crushed his spirit. He gave serious consideration to leaving the ministry. One day a friend gave Ray a poem to read in the hope that it would give him strength to live again. The inspirational words touched his heart, and he carried the poem with him for the rest of his life. The poem read:

> I want to let go, but I won't let go.
> There are battles to fight,
> By day and by night.
>
> I want to let go, but I won't let go.
> I'm sick, 'tis true,
> Worried and blue,
> And worn through and through,
> But I won't let go.
>
> I want to let go, but I won't let go.
> I will never yield!
> What! Be torn on the field
> And surrender my shield?
> No. I'll never let go!
>
> I want to let go, but I won't let go.
> May this be my song
> 'Mid legions of wrong—
> Oh, God, keep me strong
> That I may never let go![2]

The Lord did not divide the waters, but he gave Jeff Ray the strength to stand on the shore.

In 1873, Horatio G. Spafford planned a European trip for his family. At the last moment, because of business problems, he decided to remain in the States, but he sent his wife and daughters on the *S. S. Ville du Haver* in November, 1873. A few days later the *Ville du Haver* was struck by an English ship, *Lochearn*, and the *Ville du Haver* sank in twelve minutes. Mrs. Spafford was saved, but her four daughters perished. Upon reaching England, Mrs. Spafford cabled her husband a simple message, "Saved—alone." Immediately, Spafford left, by ship, to meet his wife. While enroute to England, he told the captain of the ship to inform him when they reached the approximate place his daughters had drowned. At the proper time, the captain informed Spafford that they were in the general vicinity where his girls had perished. Spafford walked on the deck of the ship and gazed at the sea. He reached into his pocket, pulled out a pen and paper, and wrote these words:

> When peace, like a river, attendeth my way,
> When sorrows like sea billows roll;
> Whatever my lot, thou has taught me to say,
> It is well, it is well with my soul.

Yes, if God does not divide the waters as we would wish, he will give us the strength to stand on the shore. With his help we can say, "It is well, it is well with my soul."

Notes

Chapter 1

1. Ben Haden, "Not Yet," *Changed Lives*, 1973, pp. 7-8.

Chapter 2

1. Robert H. Schuller, Personal testimony given on his TV program, "Hour of Power."

2. Schuller, *You Can Become the Person You Want to Be* (New York: Hawthorne Books, 1973), p. 145.

3. Schuller, *Move Ahead With Possibility Thinking*, p. 180.

Chapter 3

1. R. L. Middleton, *The Gift of Love* (Nashville: Broadman Press, 1976), p. 15.

2. Tupelo *Journal*, January 8, 1978.

3. A. Leonard Griffith, *Beneath the Cross of Jesus* (Nashville: Abingdon Press, 1961), p. 18.

Chapter 4

1. William Shakespeare, *Macbeth*, Act V, Scene III, lines 39-45.

Chapter 5

1. Madeline S. Miller and J. Lane Miller, *Harper's Bible Dictionary* (New York: Harper and Row, 1952), p. 443.

2. James D. Mallory, *The Kink and I* (Santa Anna, California: Victor Books, 1973), pp. 83-127.

Chapter 6

1. *The Commission*, January, 1978.

Chapter 8

1. Bill Stephens, editor, *Modern Stories of Inspiration* (Nashville: Broadman Press, 1975), pp. 9-10.

2. Ibid., p. 68.

Chapter 9

1. Harold G. Warlick, Jr., *Liberation from Guilt* (Nashville: Broadman Press, 1976), p. 65.

Chapter 10

1. Dale Carnegie, *How to Win Friends and Influence People* (New York: Pocket Books, 1936), p. 79.

Chapter 13

1. "Positive People," *Creative Help for Daily Living* (June, 1977, Vol. 28/No. 5), pp. 6-7.

Chapter 14

1. Judith Viorst, *Redbook*, February 1975.

2. Ibid.

3. Muriel James, *Born to Win* (Reading, Massachusetts: Addison-Wesley, 1971), p. 51.

4. Marabel Morgan, *The Total Woman* (Old Tappan, New Jersey: Fleming H. Revell, 1973), p. 62.

5. Ibid., p. 63.

6. Viorst, *Redbook*, February 1975.

7. Ibid.

8. Fred M. Wood, *Growing a Life Together* (Nashville: Broadman Press, 1975), p. 117.

9. Joyce Landorff, *Tough and Tender* (Old Tappan, New Jersey: Fleming H. Revell, 1975), p. 61.

Chapter 15

1. James Dobson, *Hide or Seek* (Old Tappan, New Jersey: Fleming H. Revell, 1974), p. 25.

2. Luther B. Bridgers, "He Keeps Me Singing."

Chapter 17

1. Norman Vincent Peale, "How to Let Go All Worry Thoughts," *Creative Help for Daily Living* (July, 1977, Vol. 28, No. 6), pp. 9-10.

2. *Proclaim* (January, February, March 1978), p. 9.